FOOD STALL
Coloring Book

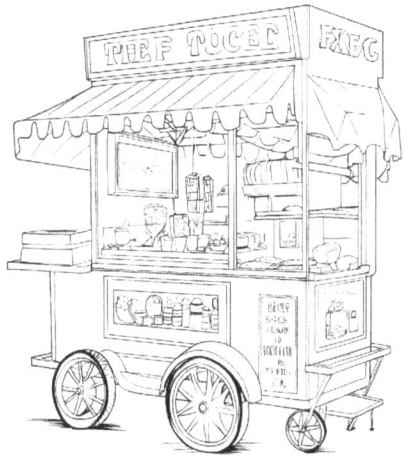

Discover a world of taste with the 'Food Stall Coloring Book'! Dive into the vibrant and delicious world of global street food with 50 unique single-sided coloring pages. Immerse yourself in the colorful markets, capture the essence of street food vendors, and learn about the cultural significance of each country. Whether you're a painting enthusiast or a food lover, this book is a delicious blend of art and culinary discovery. Immerse yourself in the art of coloring as you bring this beautiful food stall to life with your creativity.

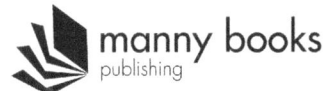

manny books
publishing

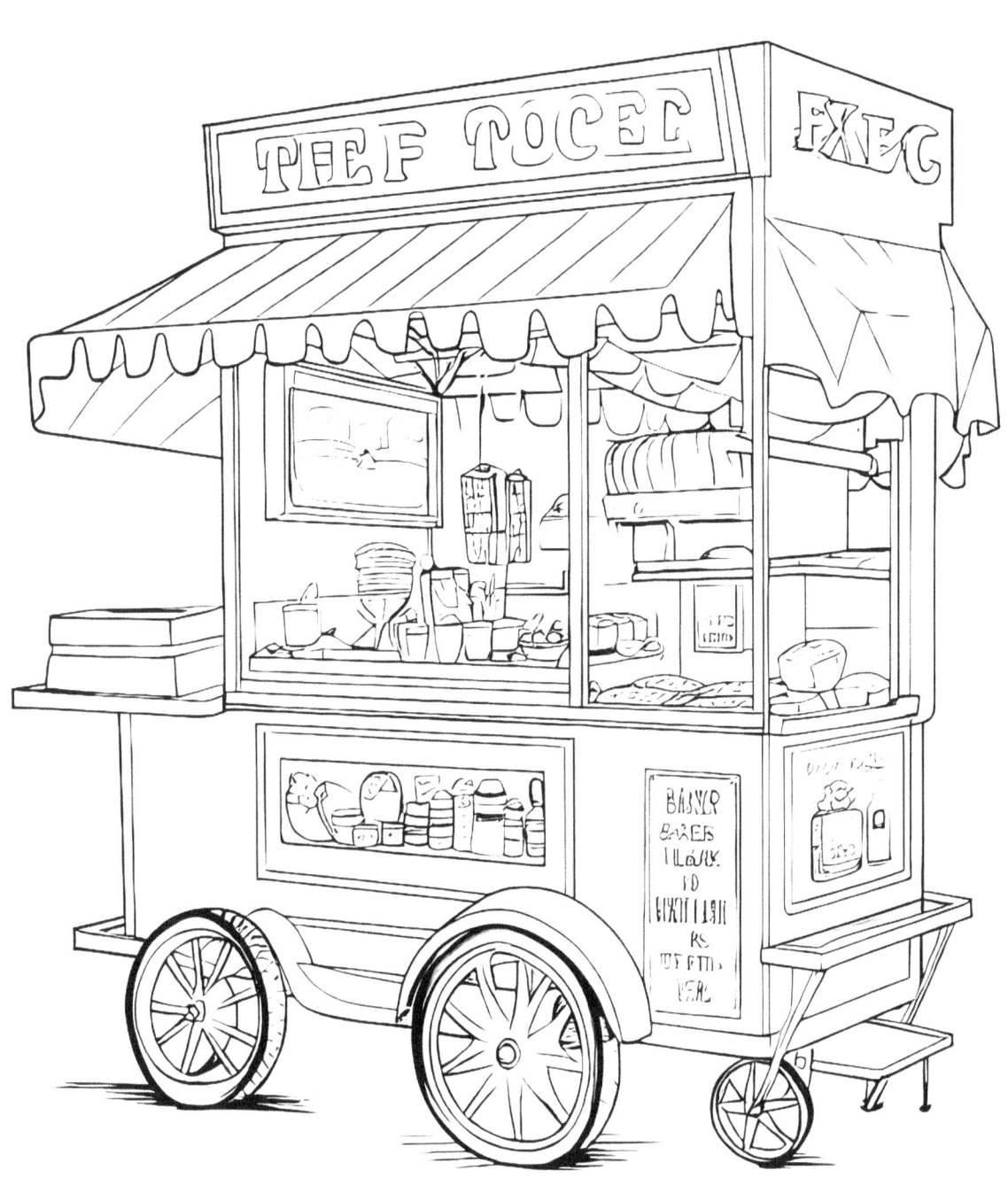

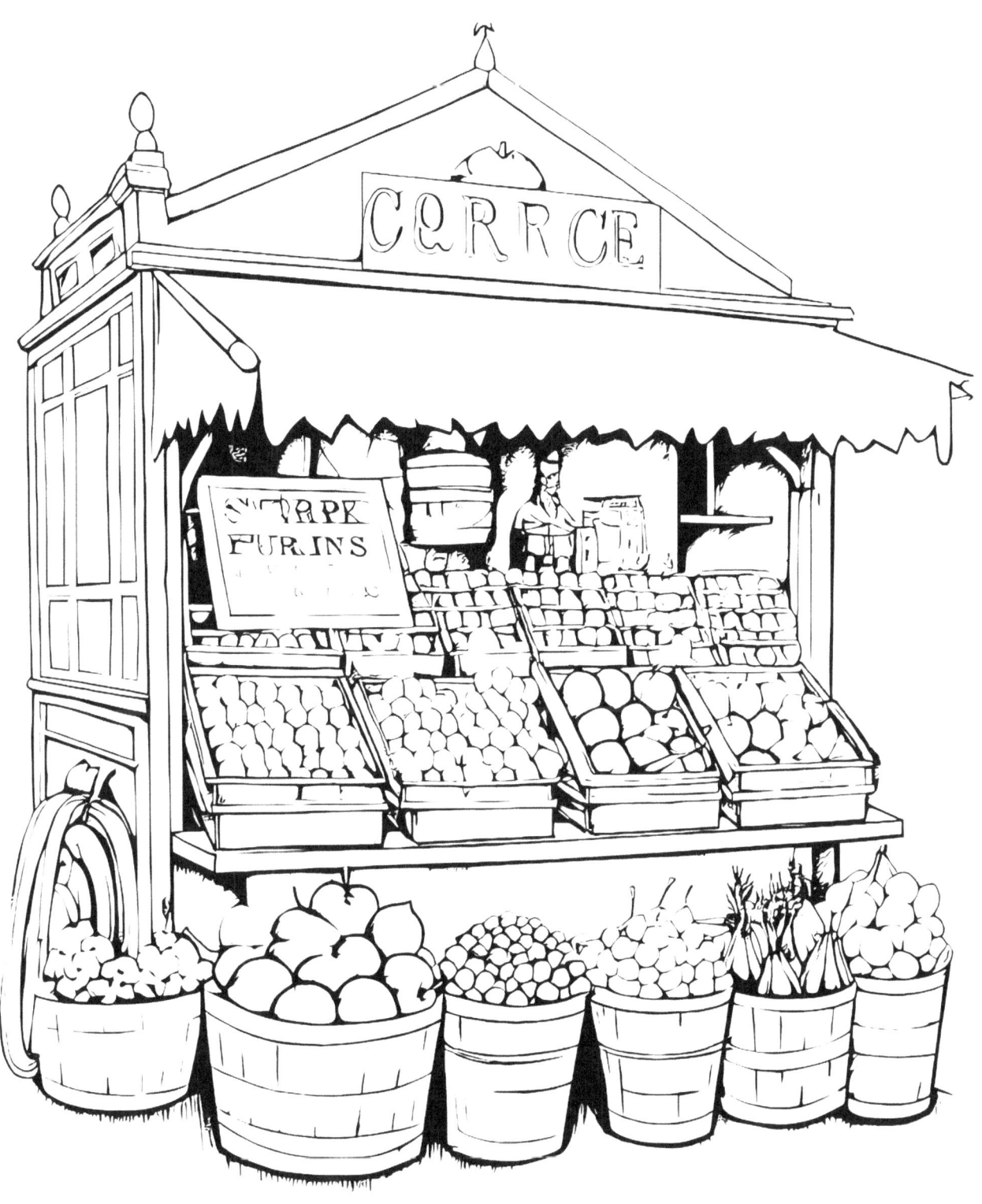

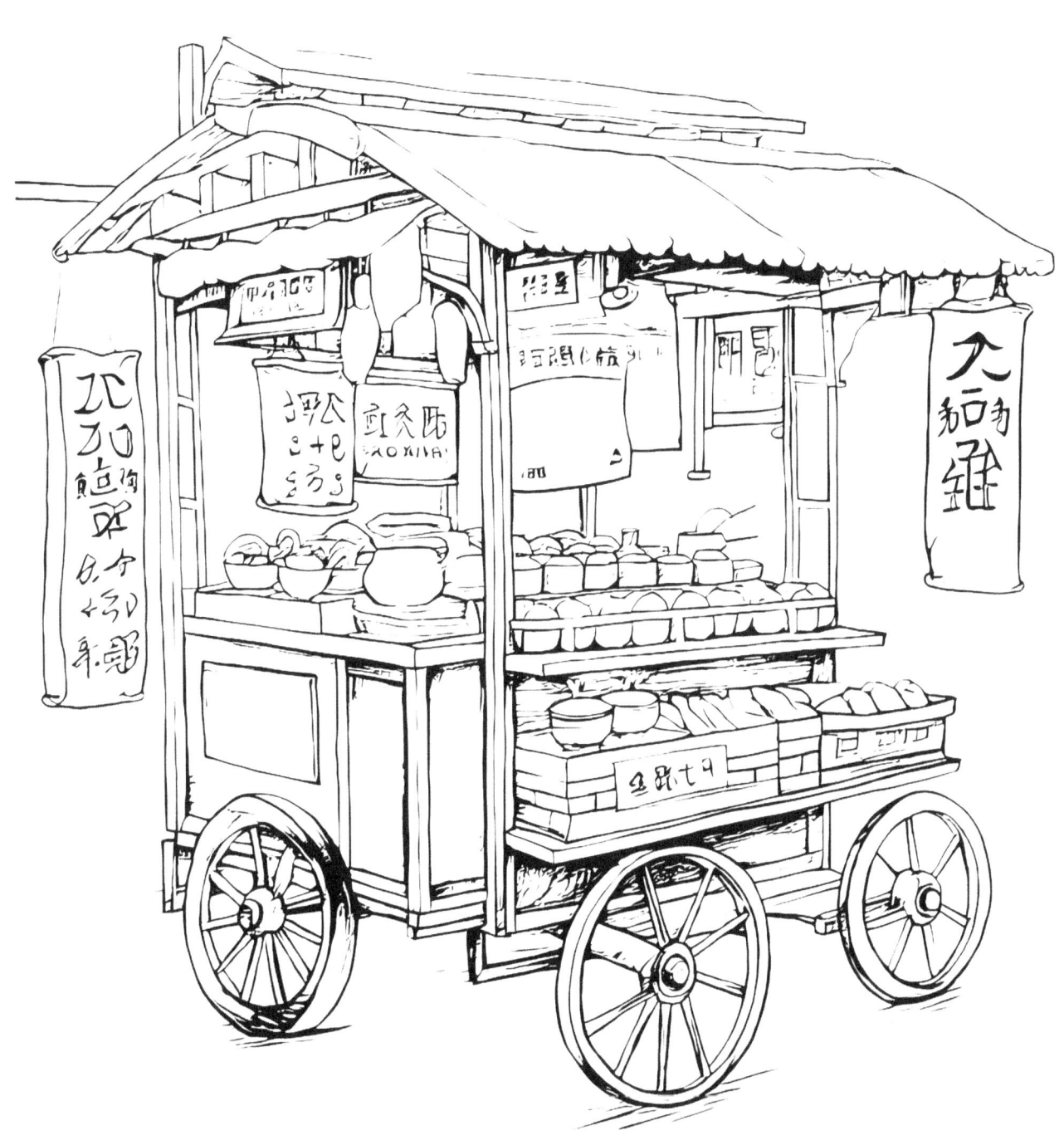

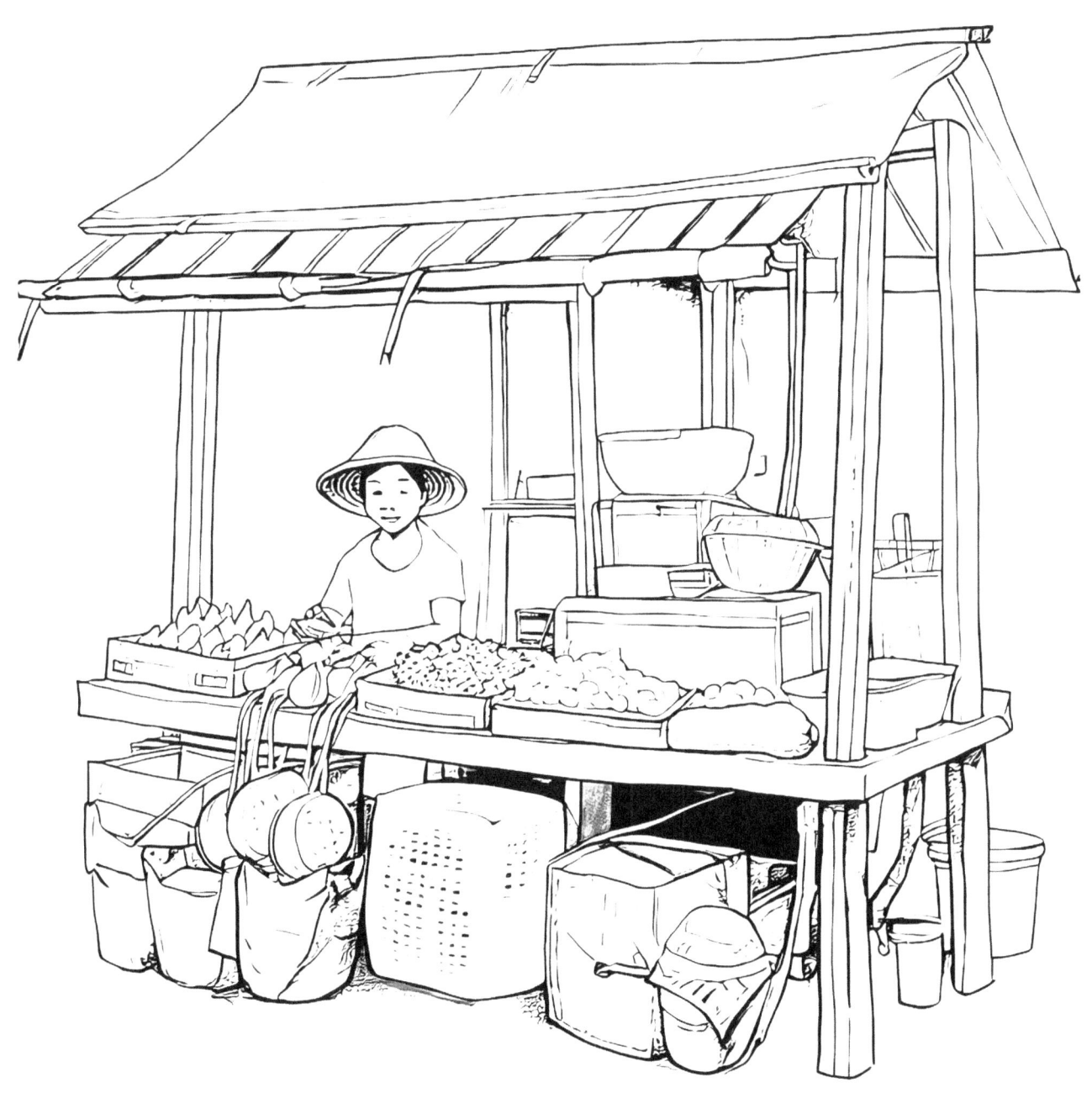

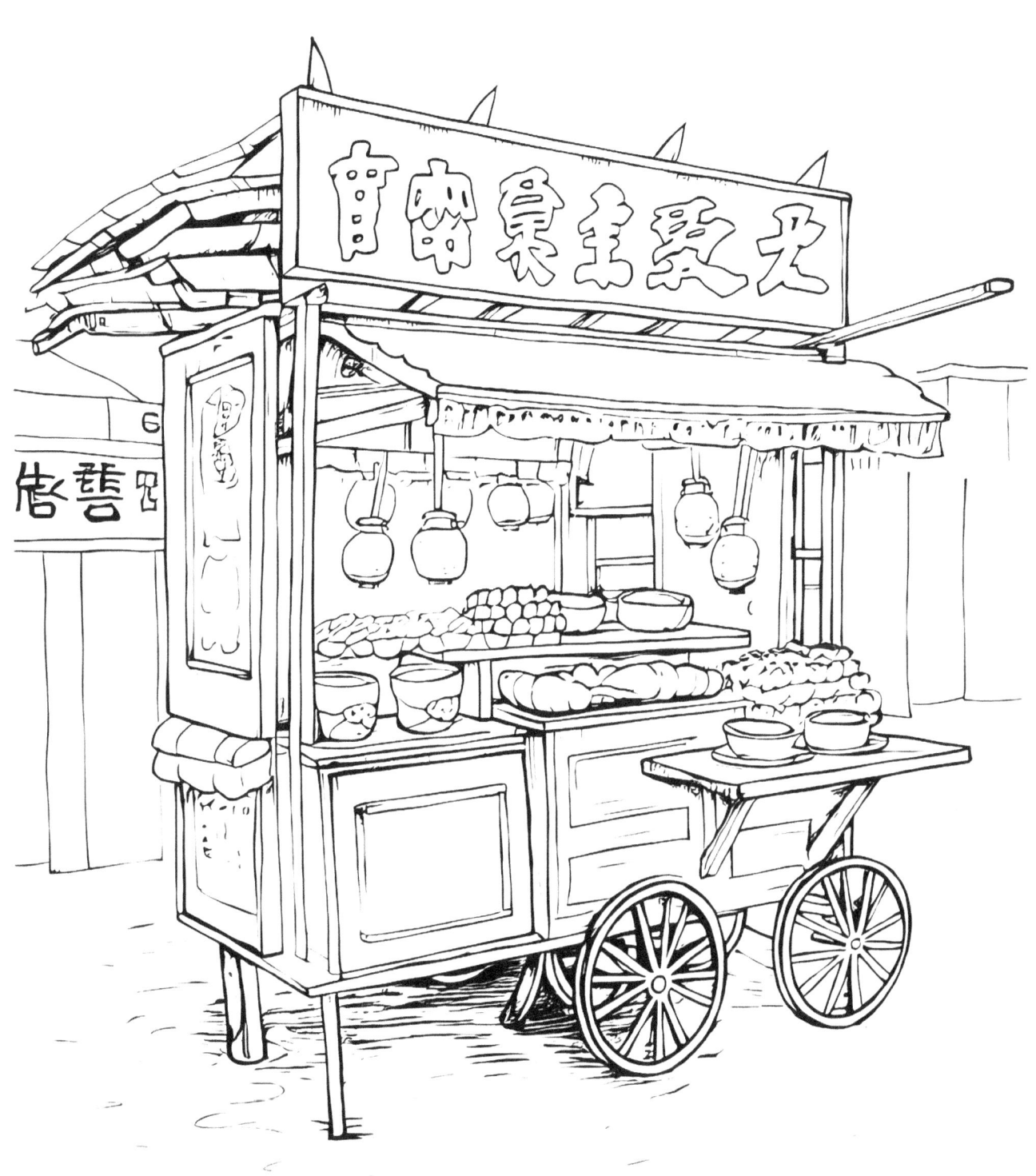

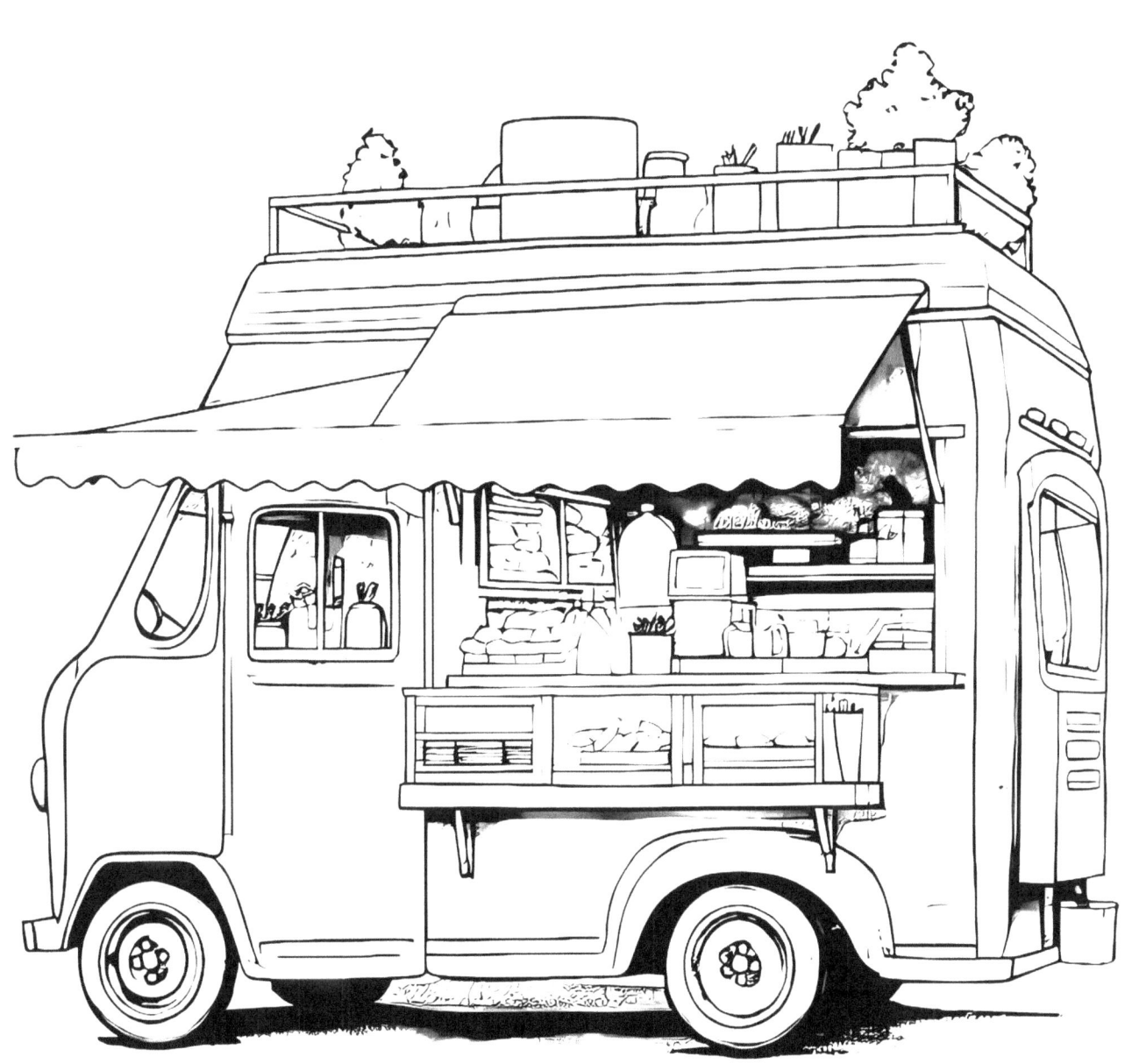

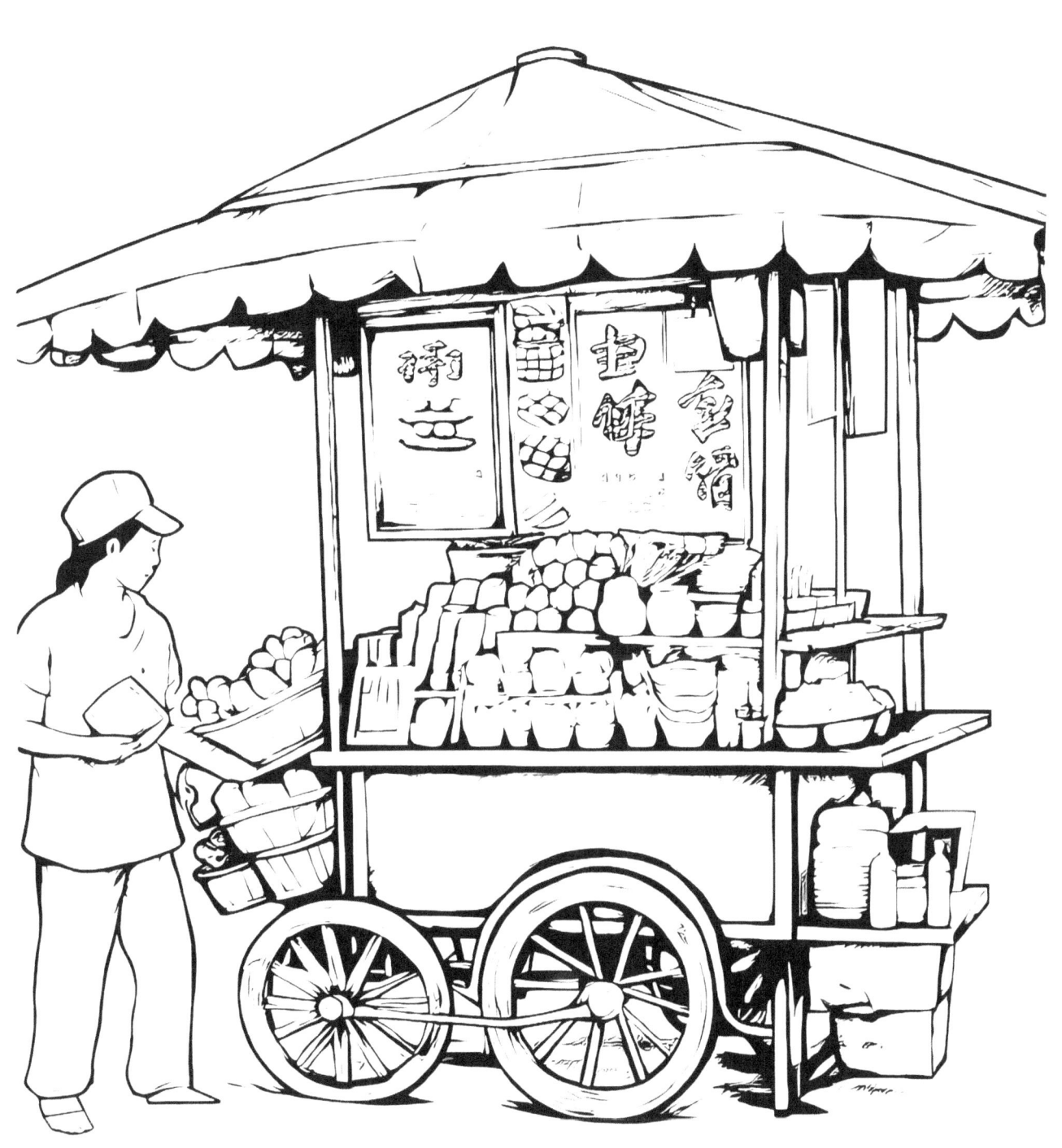

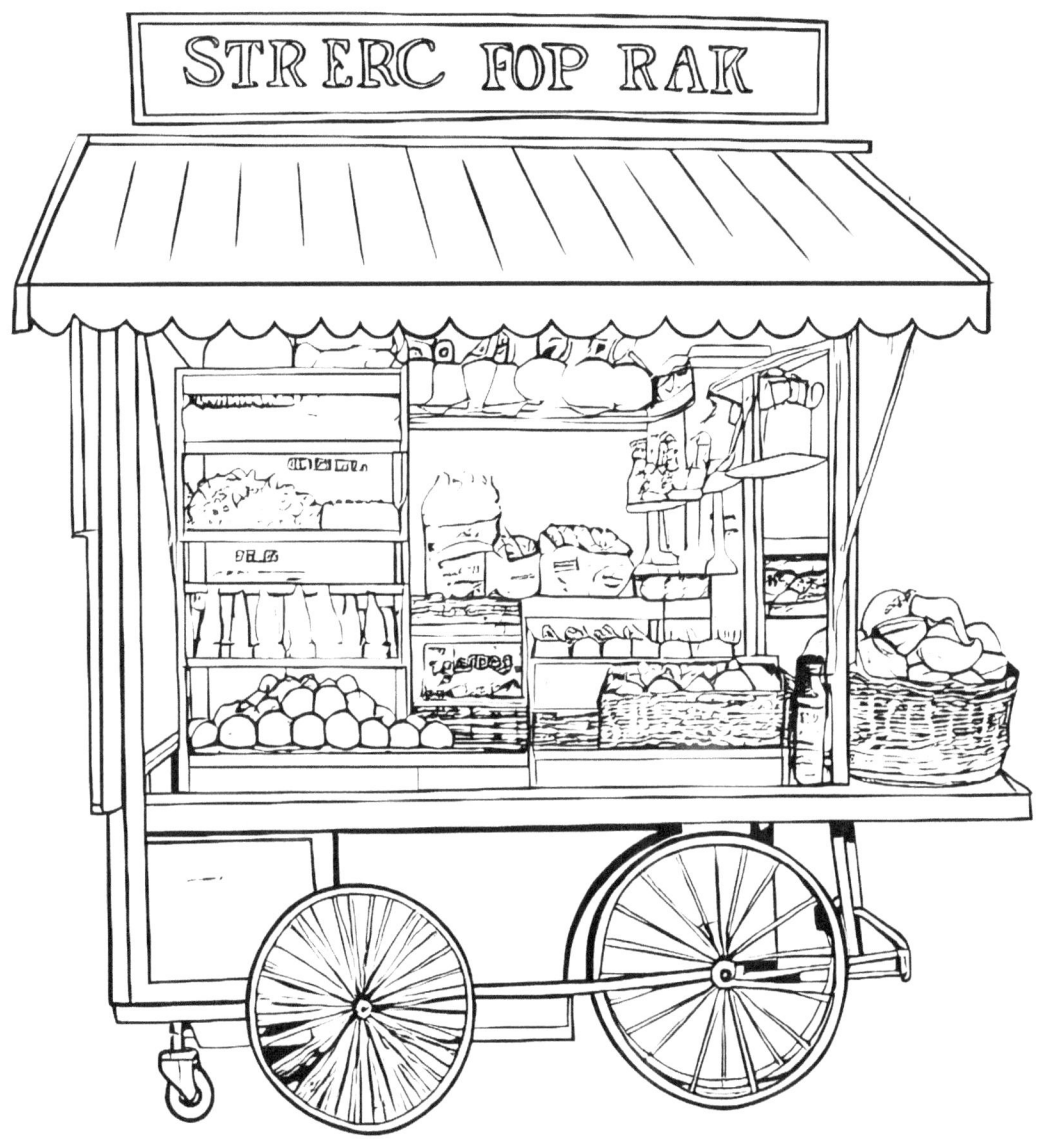

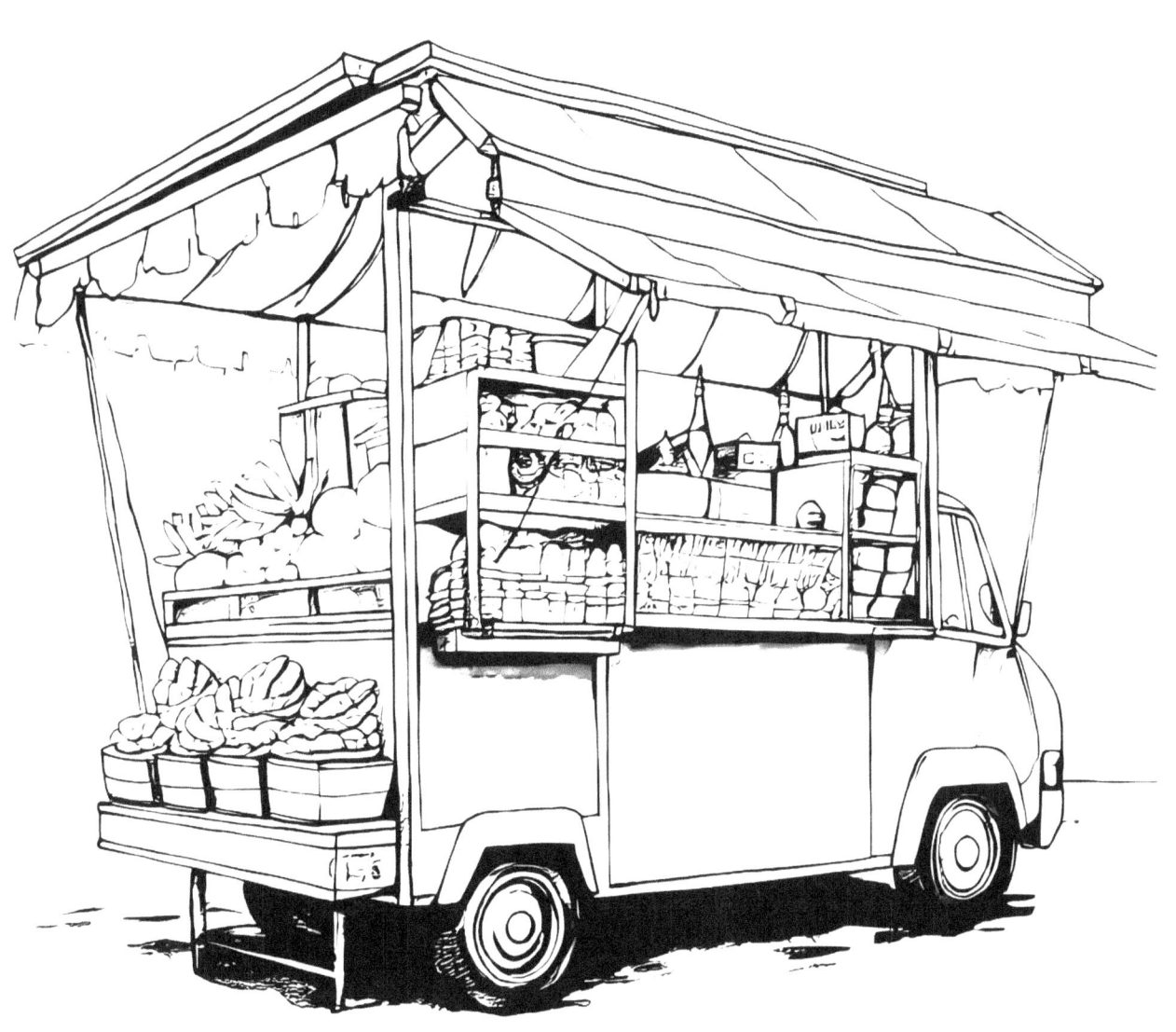

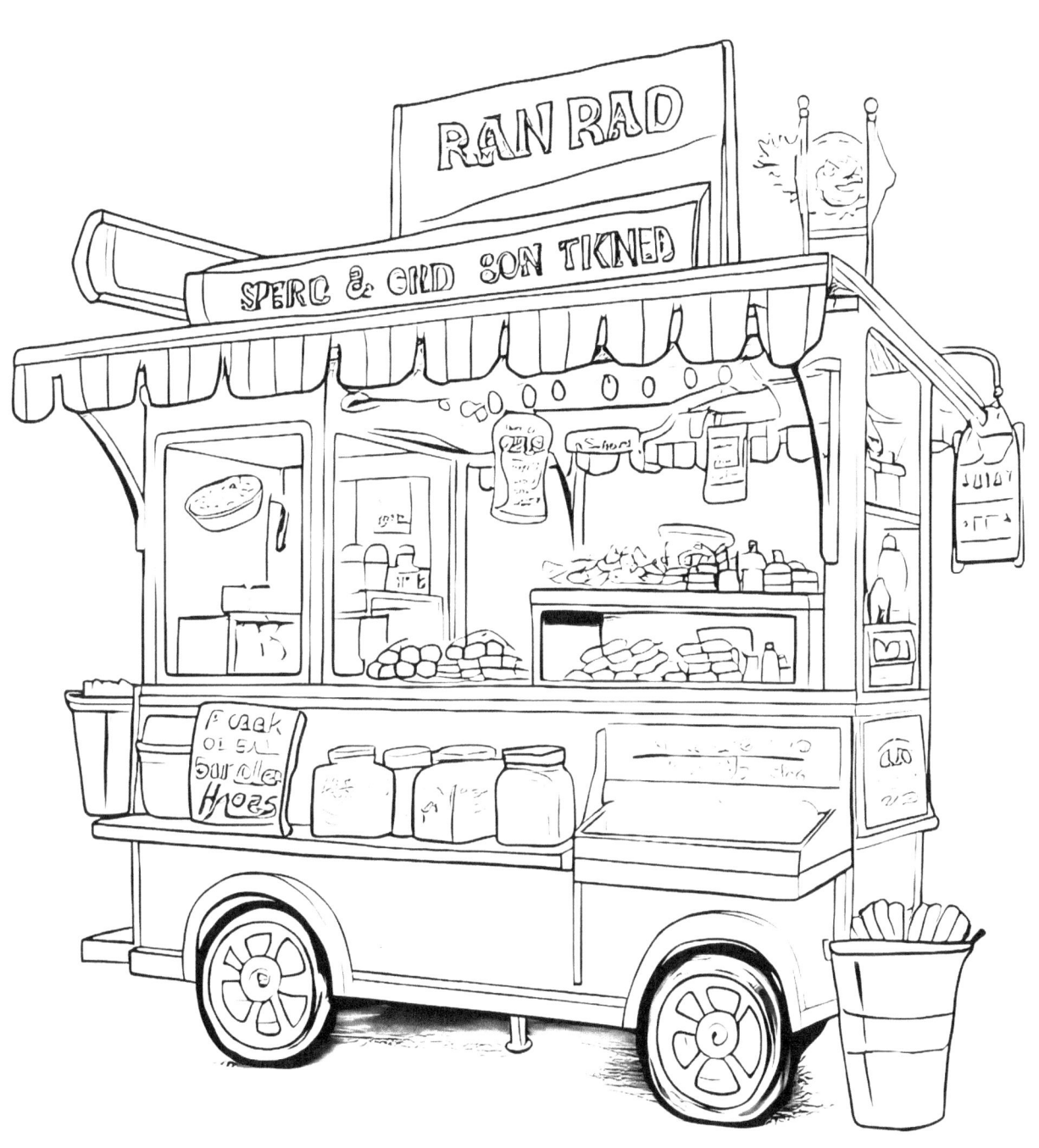

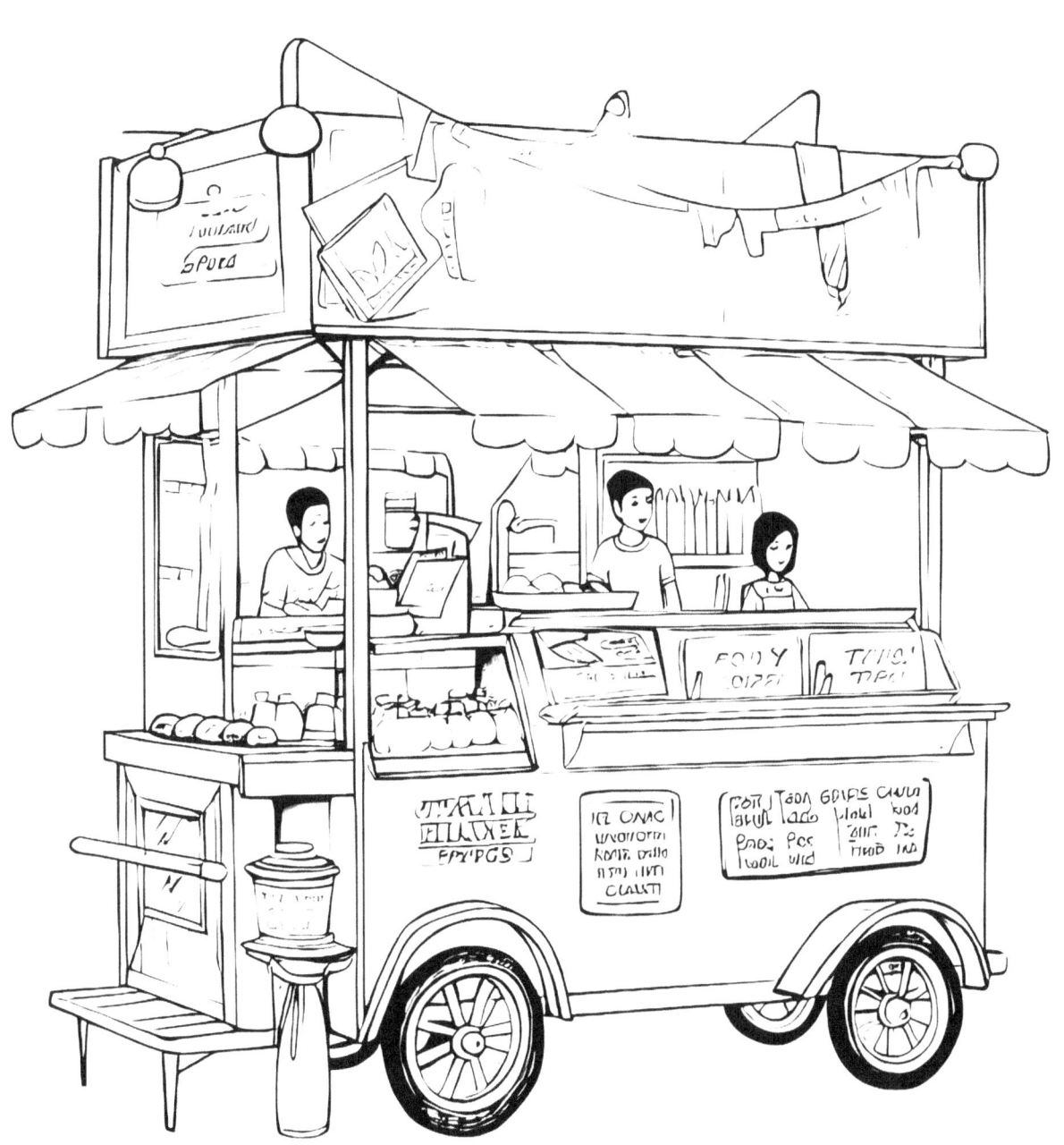

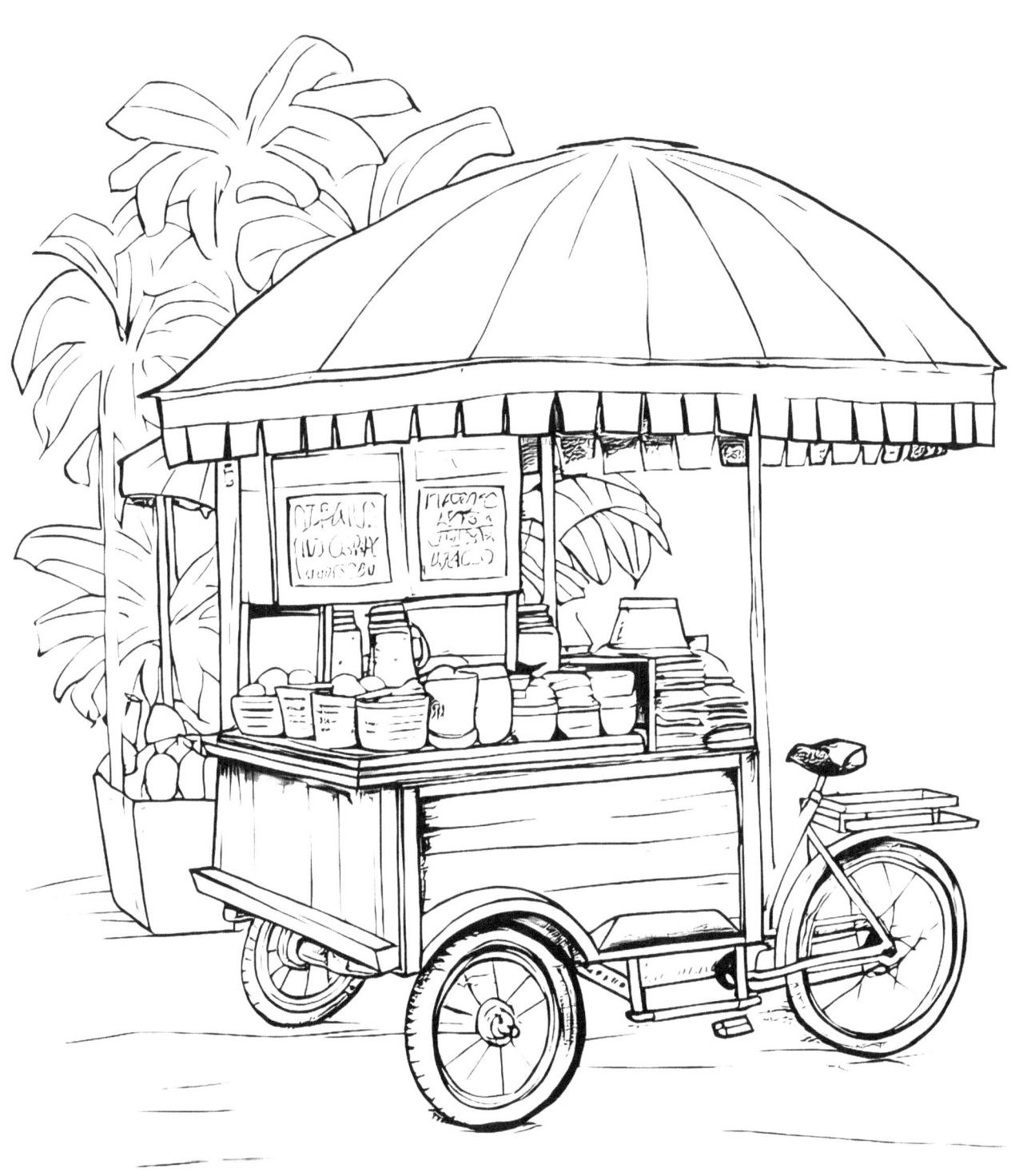

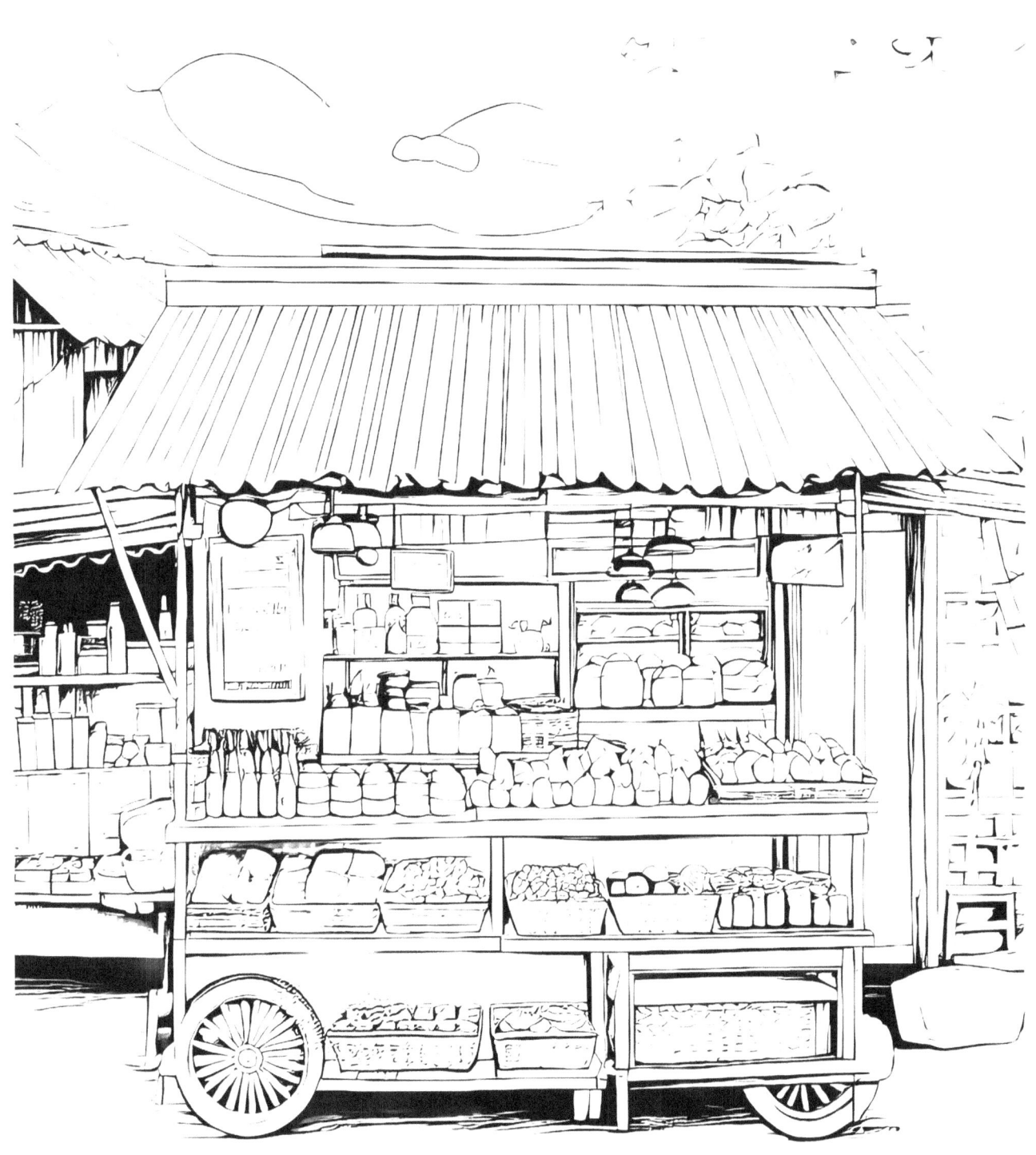

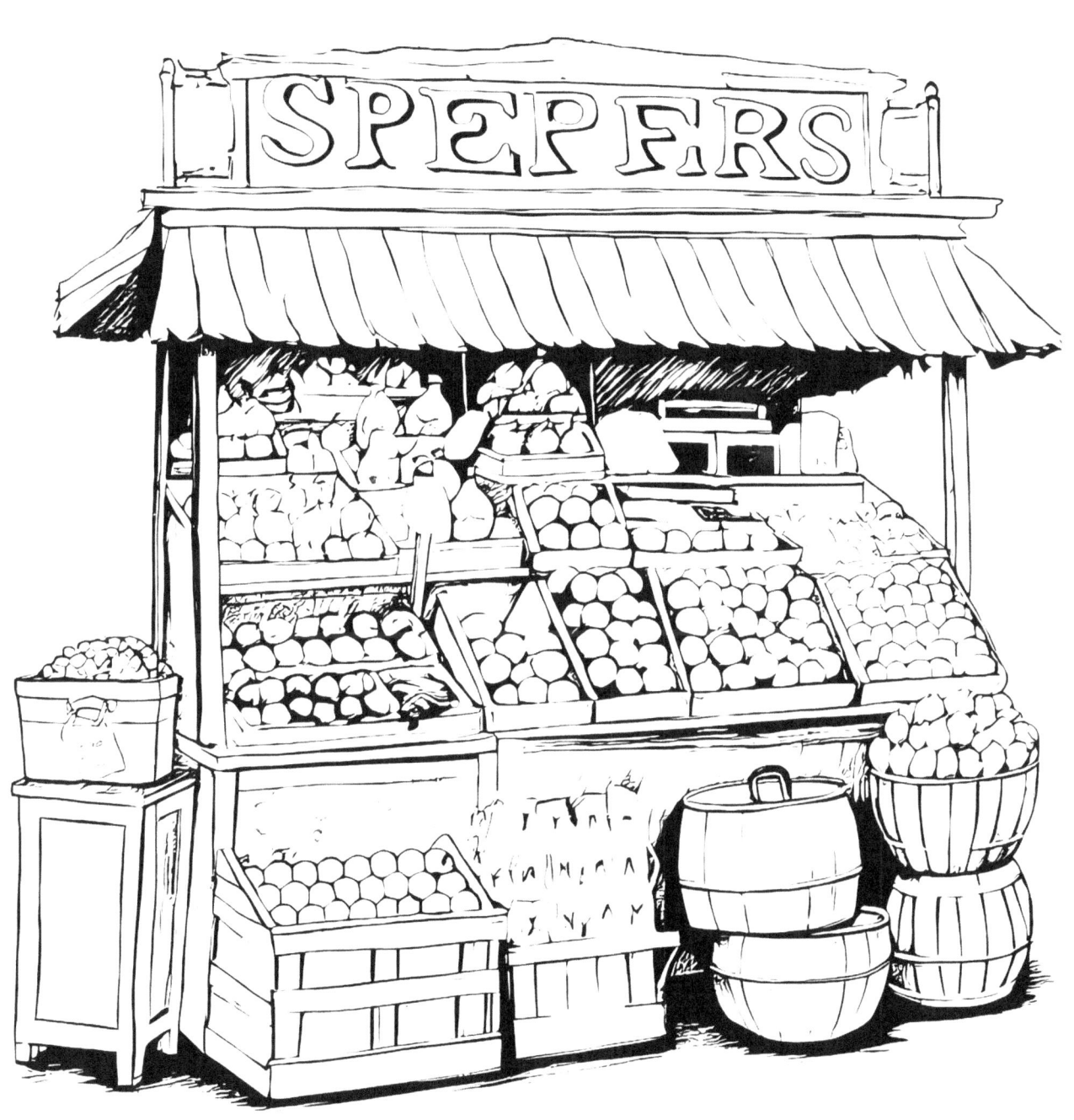

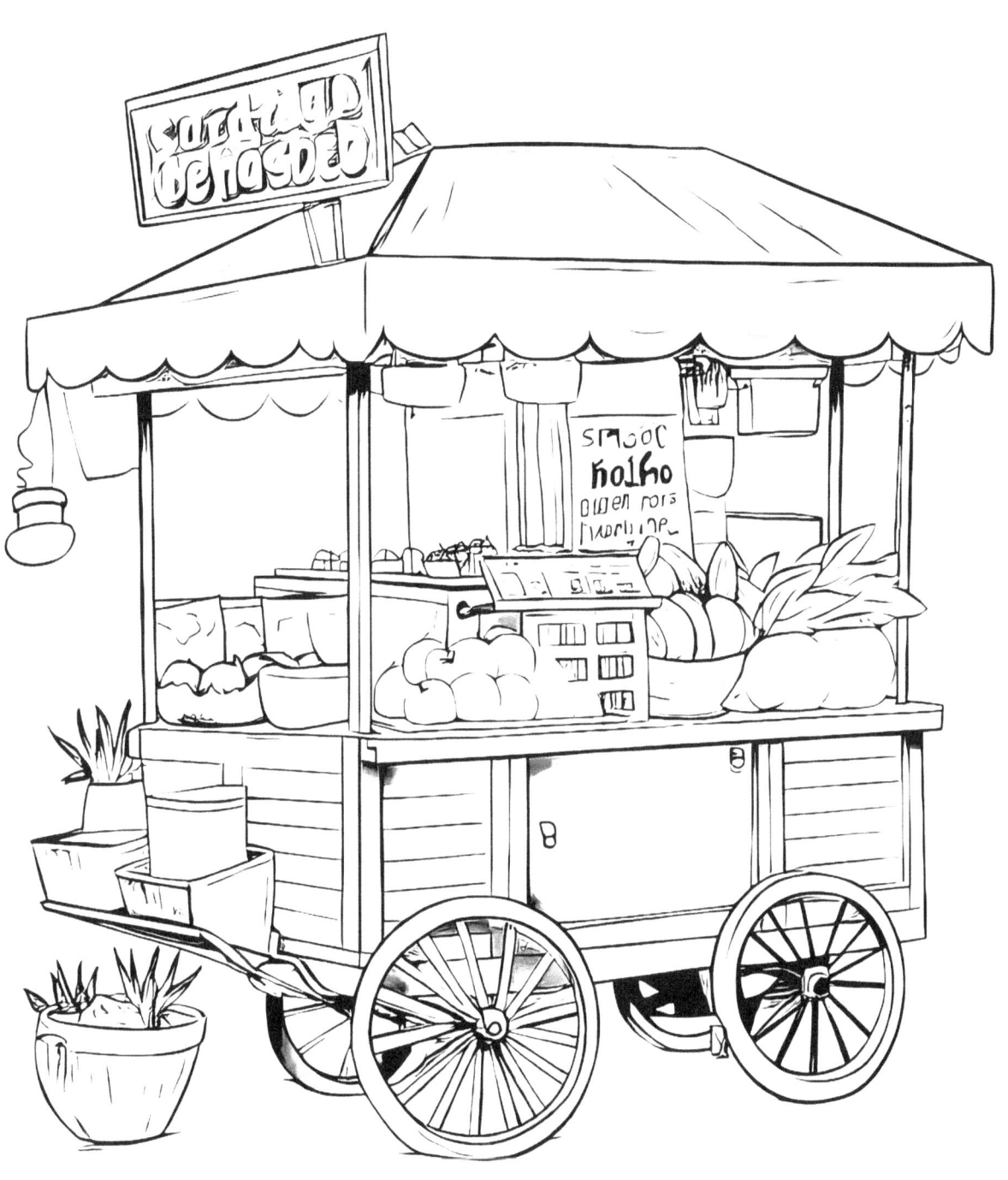

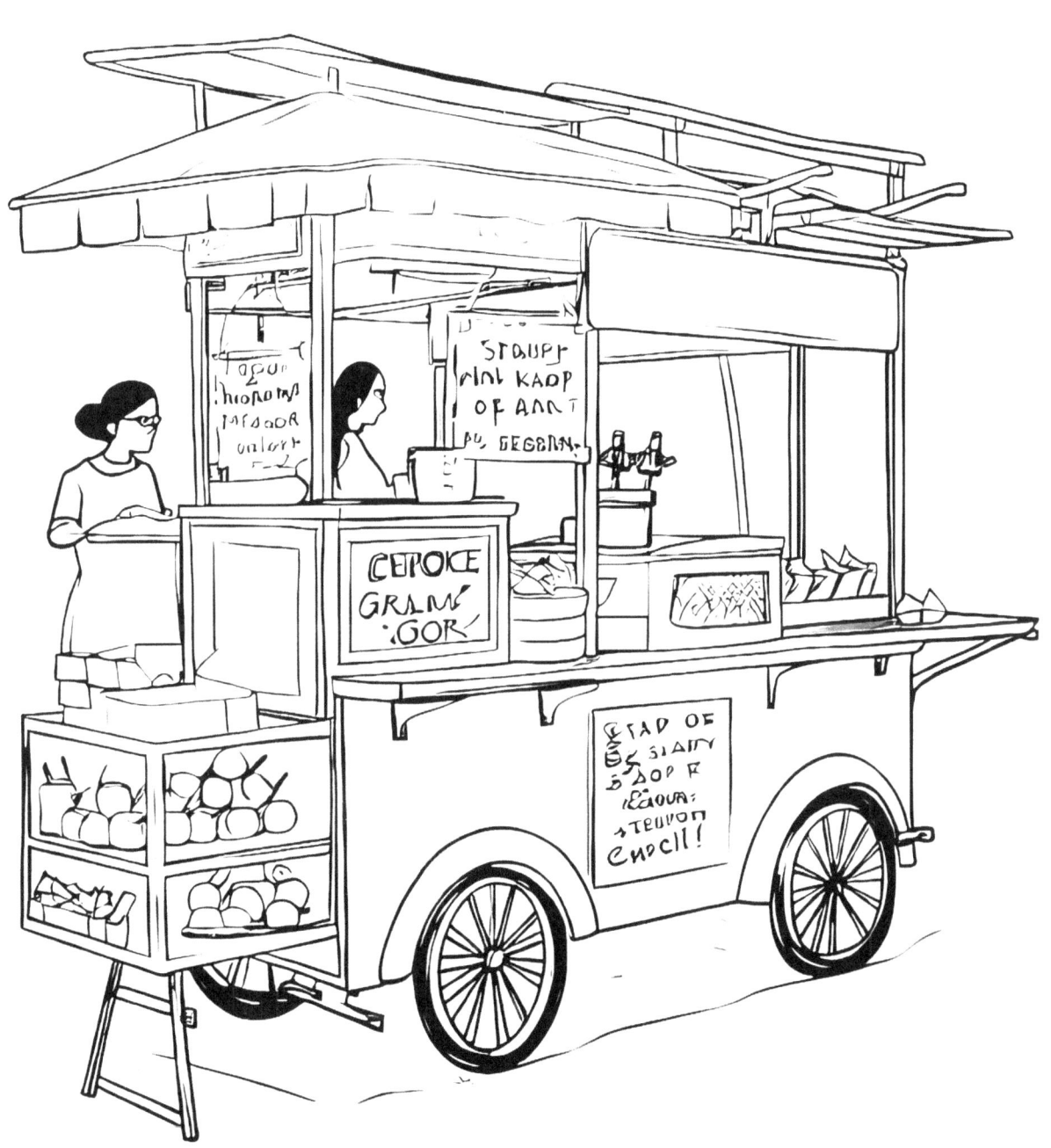

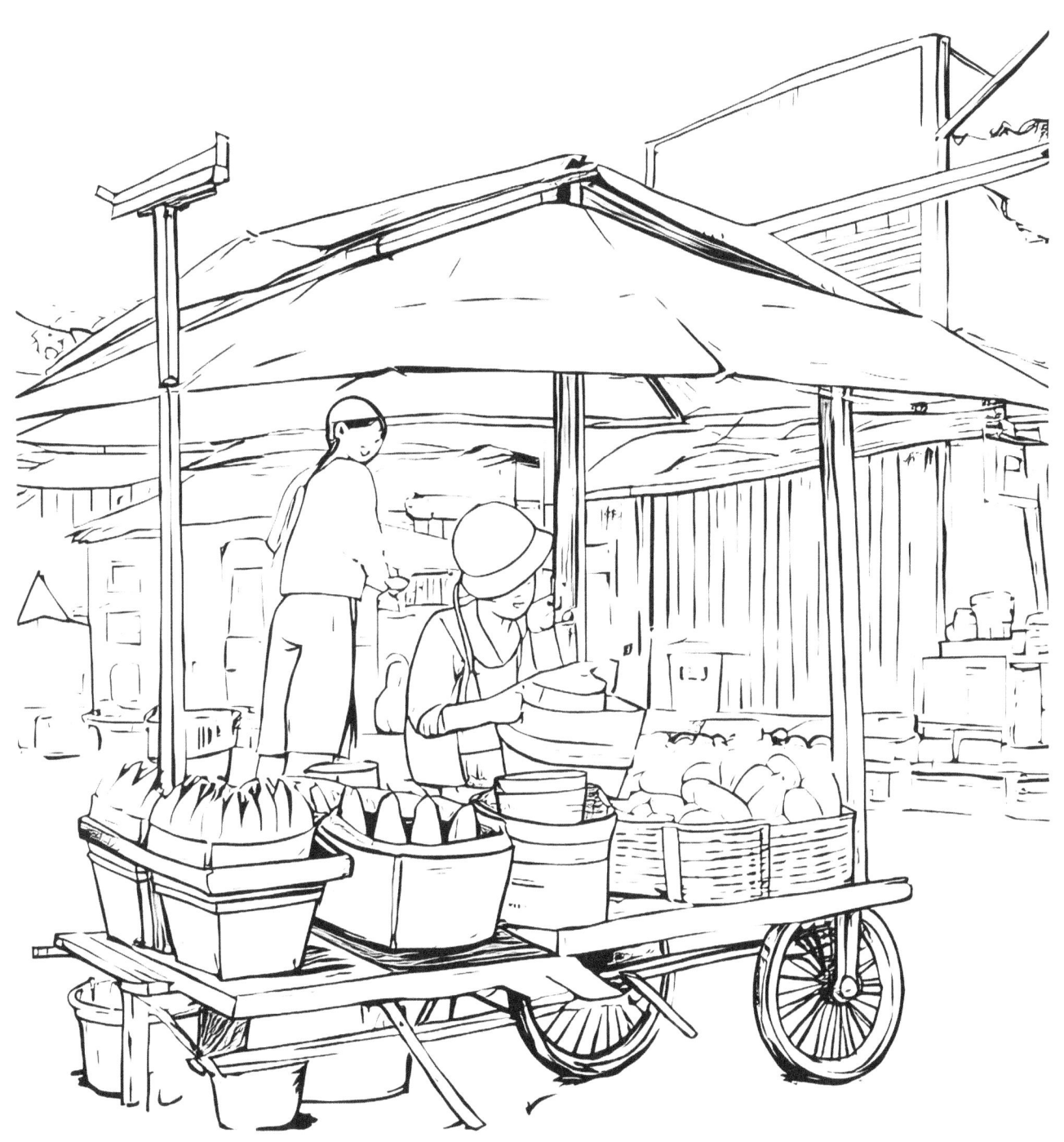

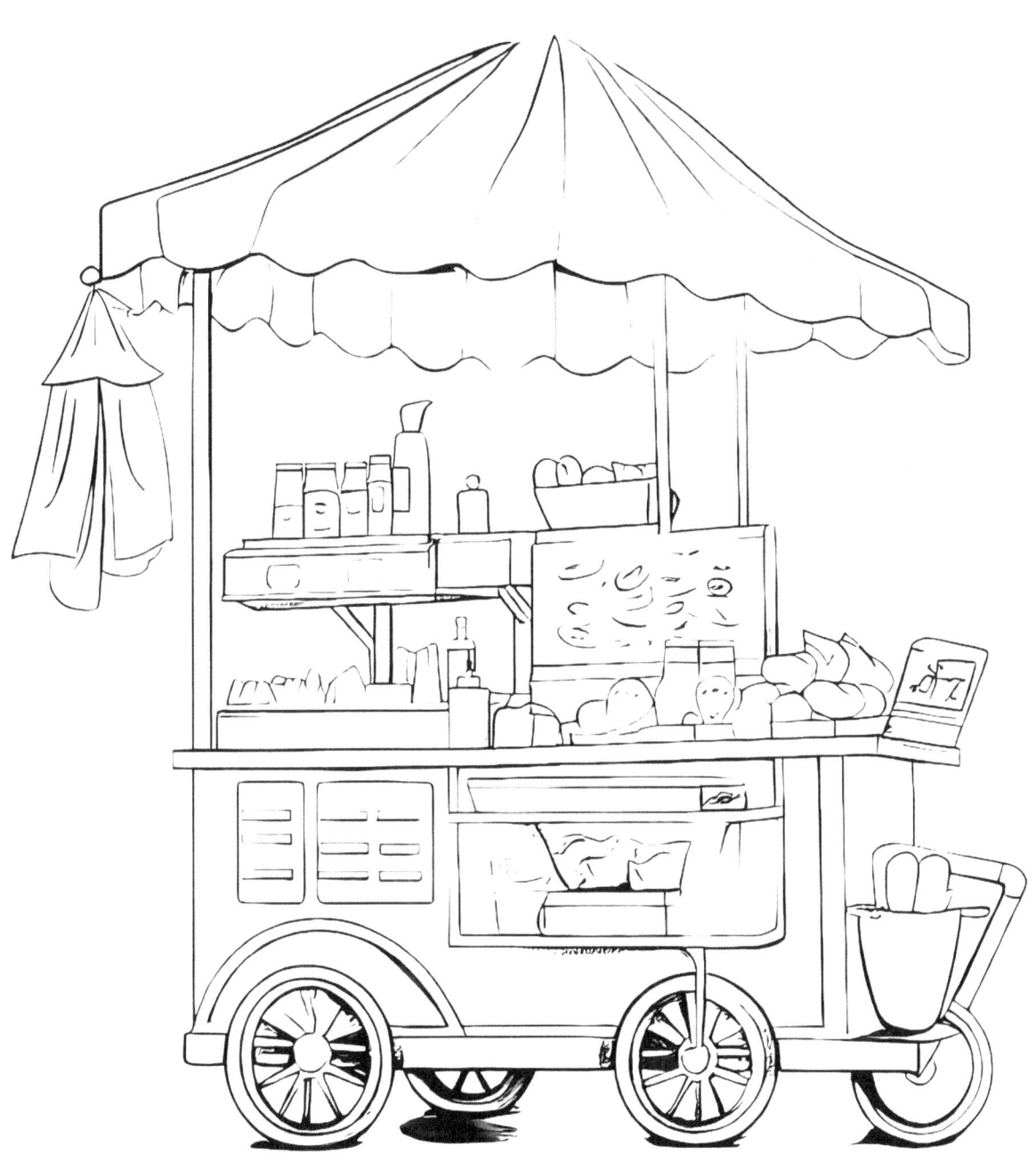

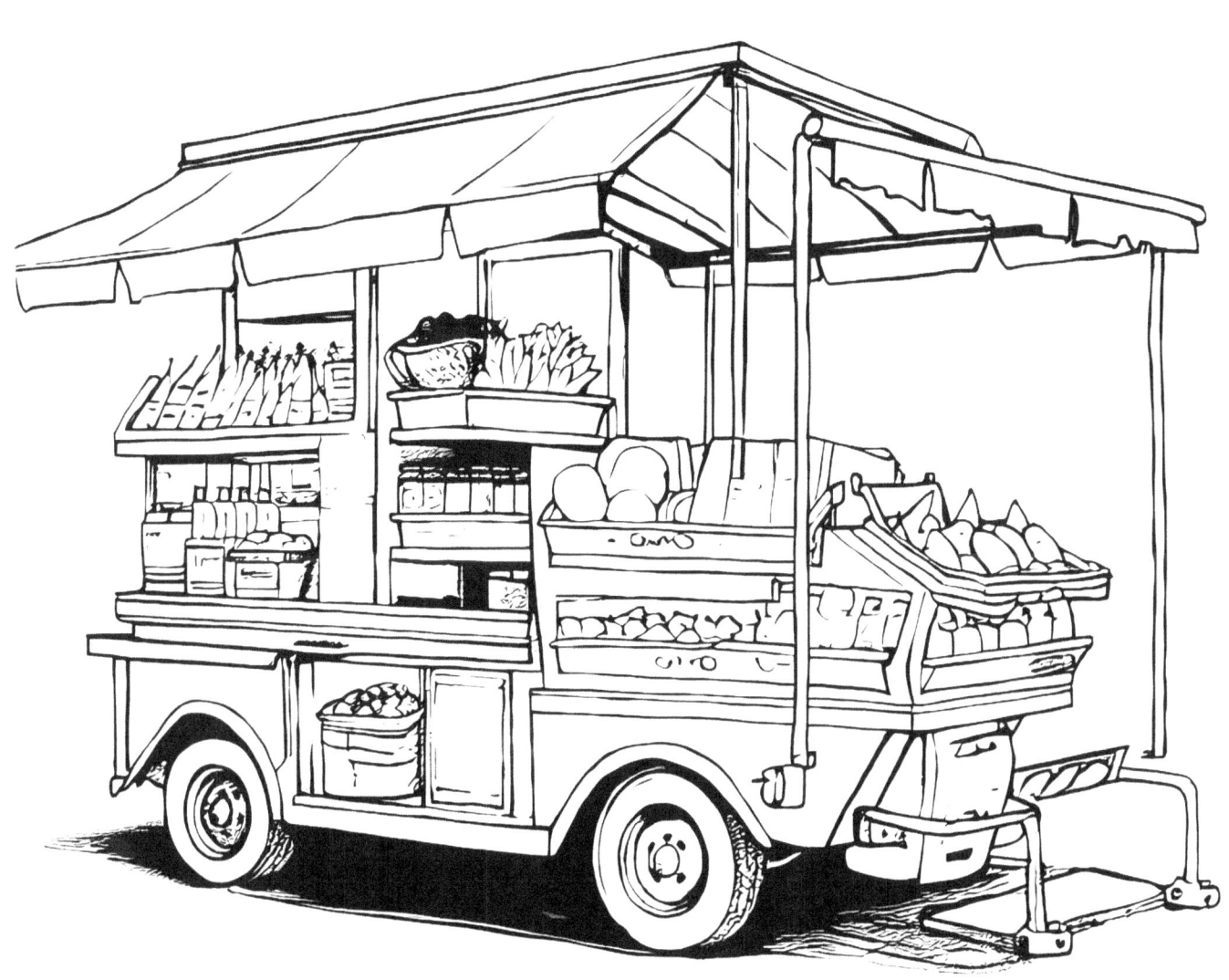

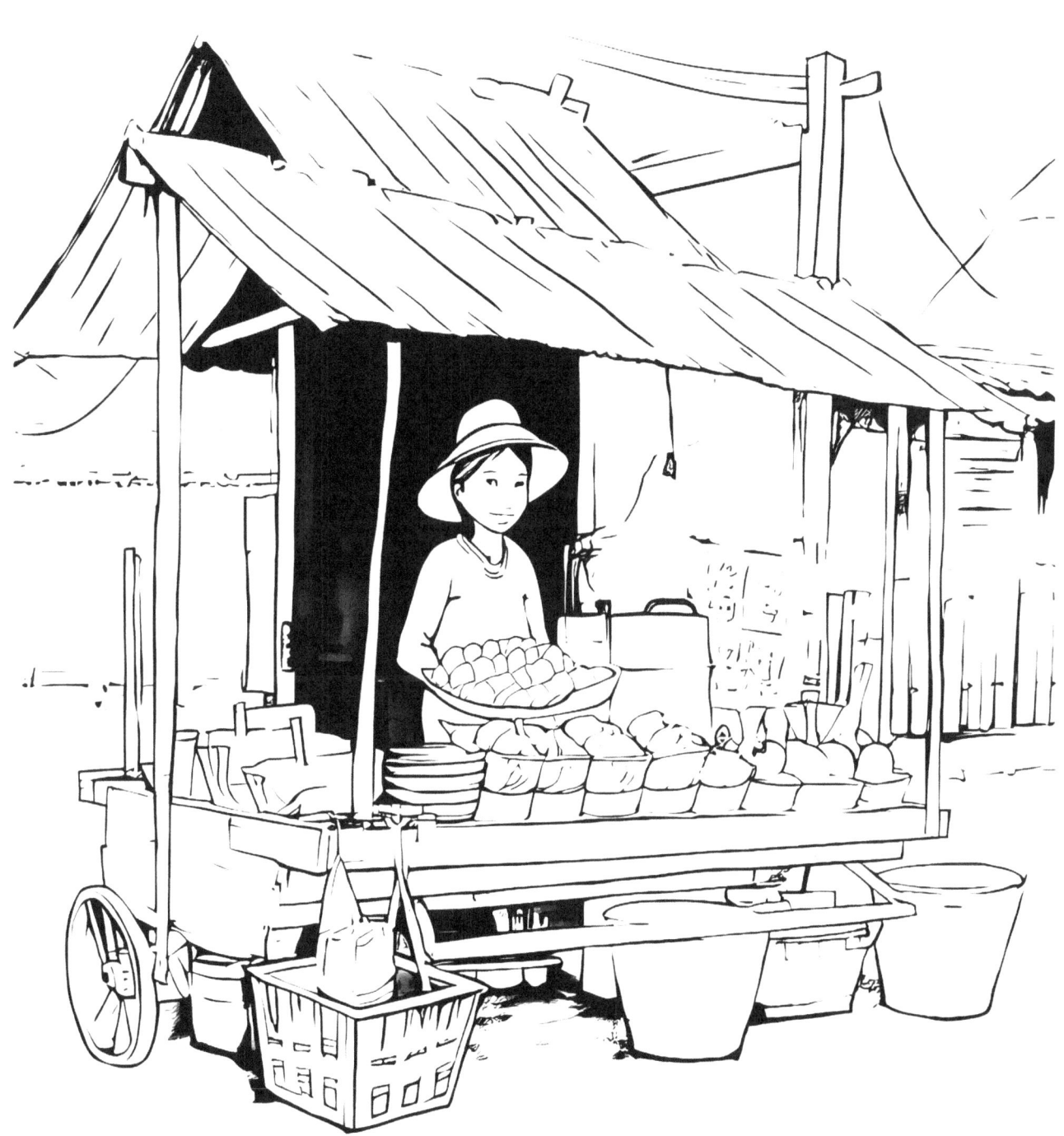

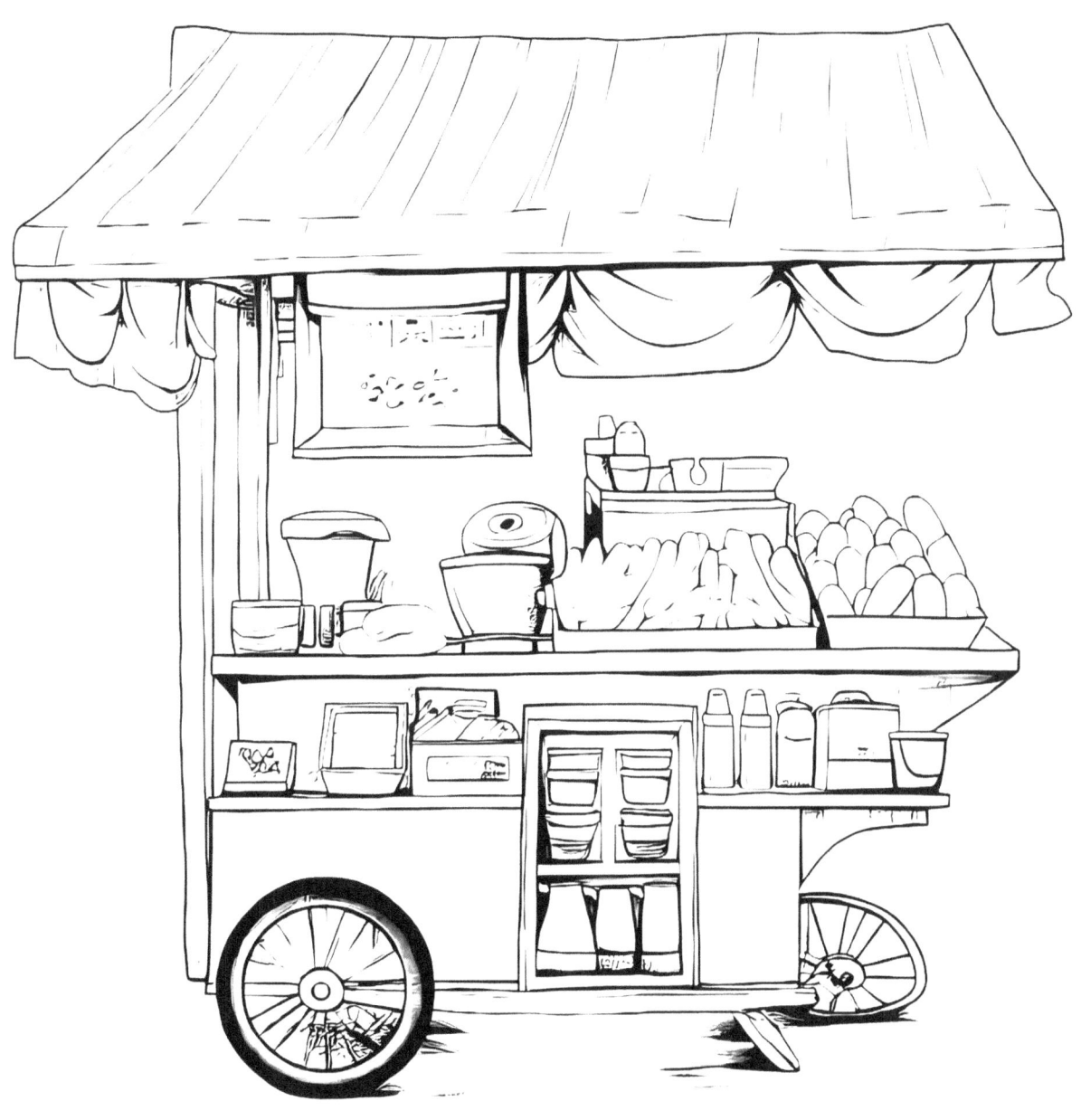

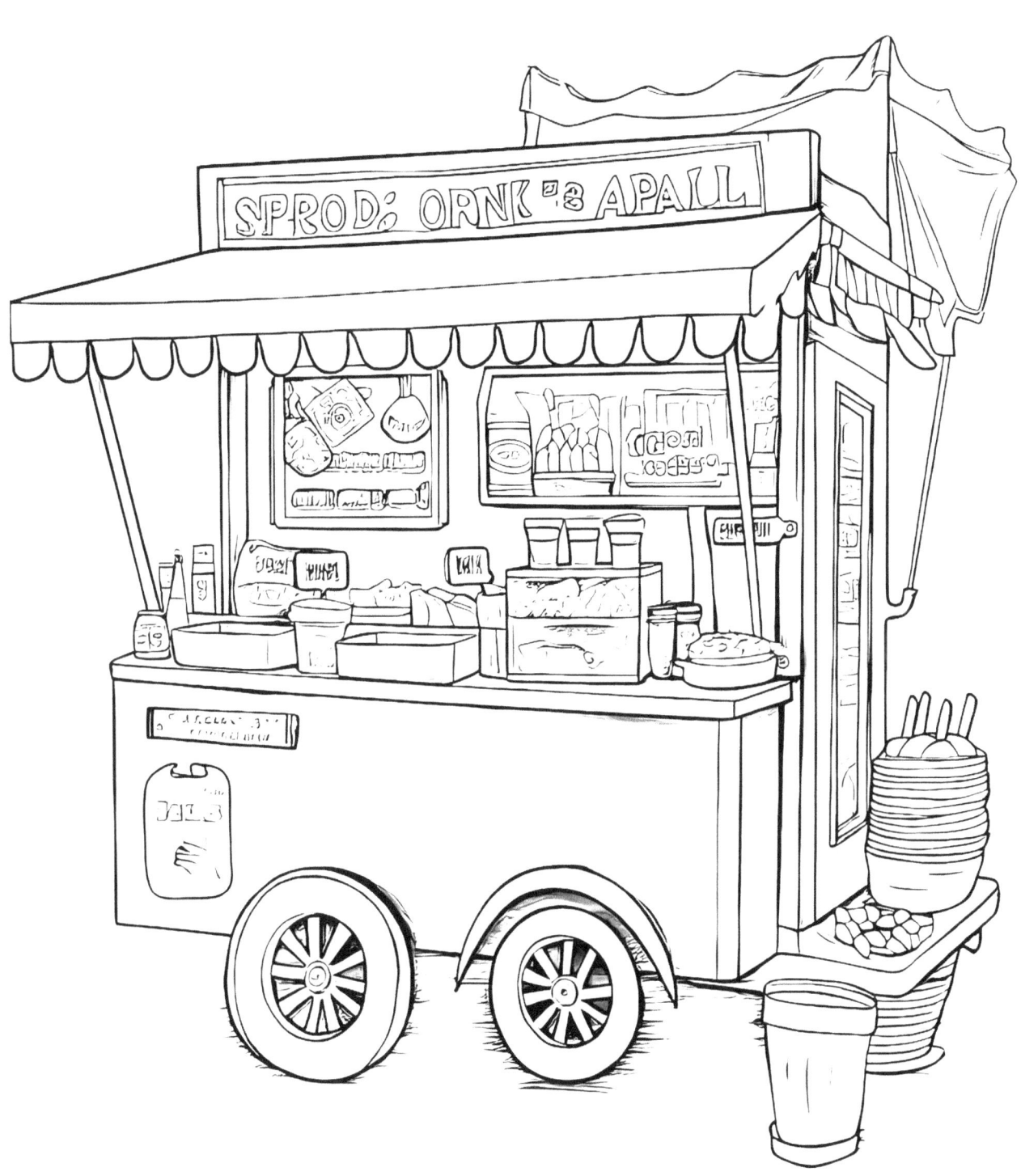

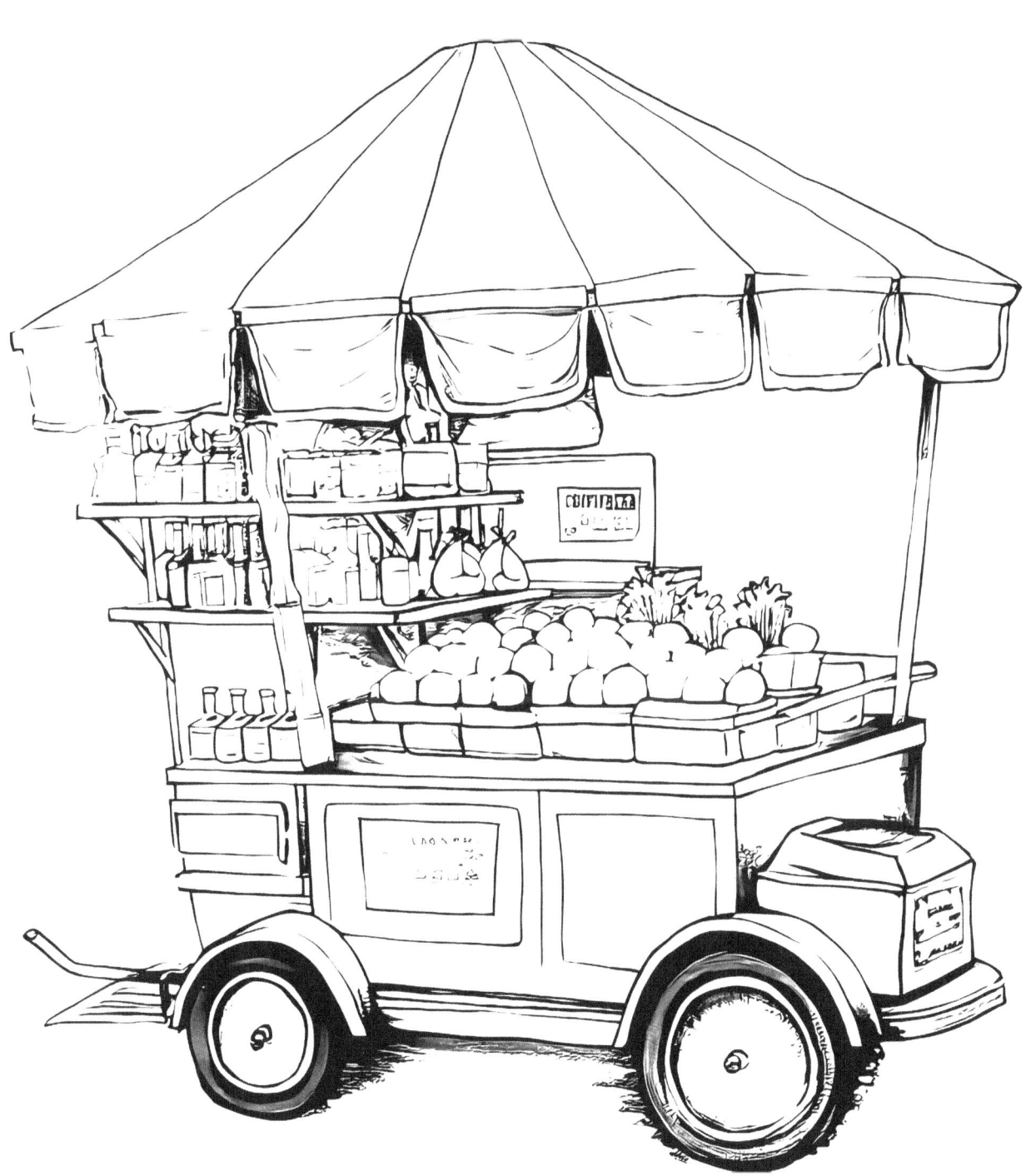

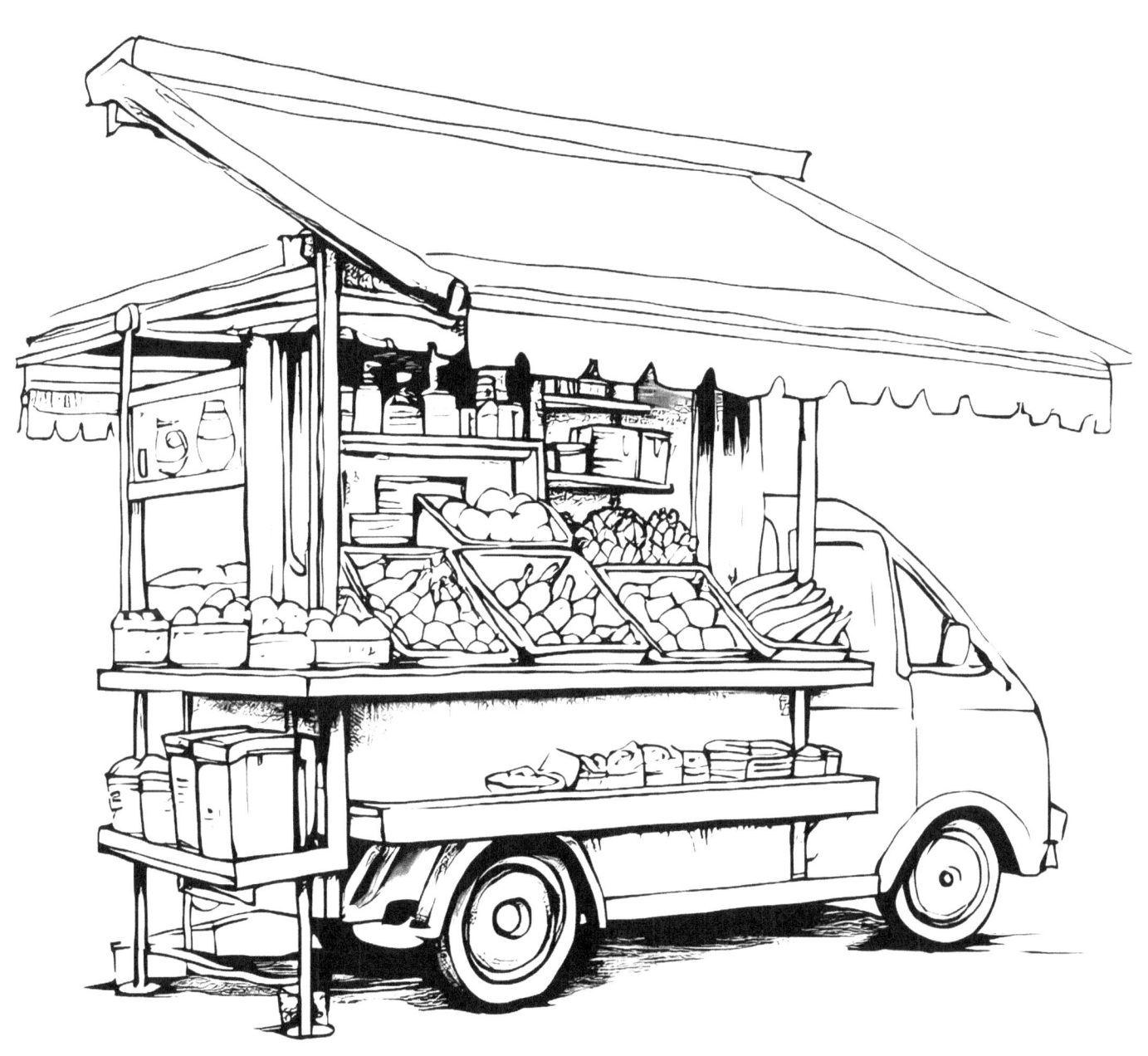

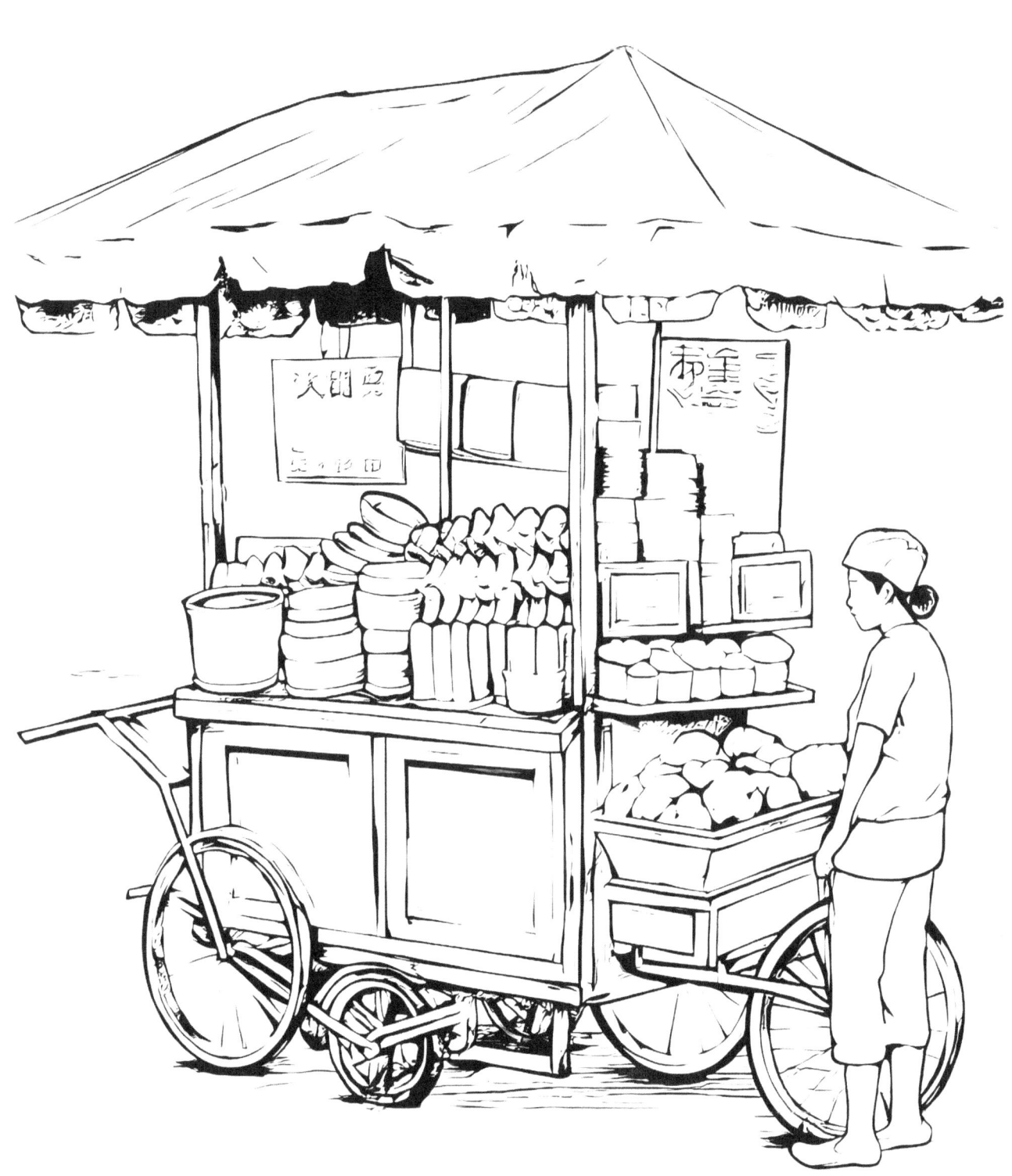

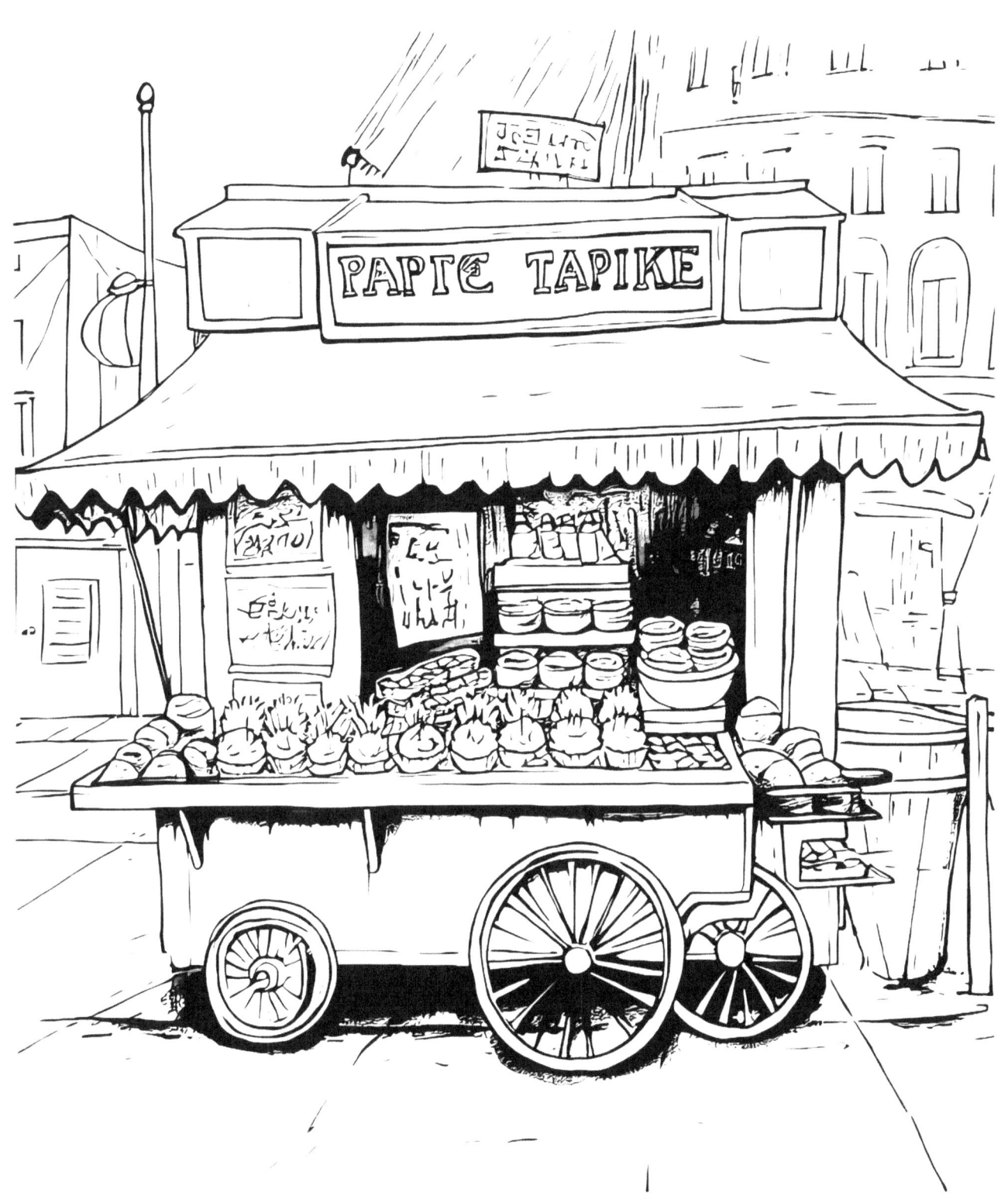

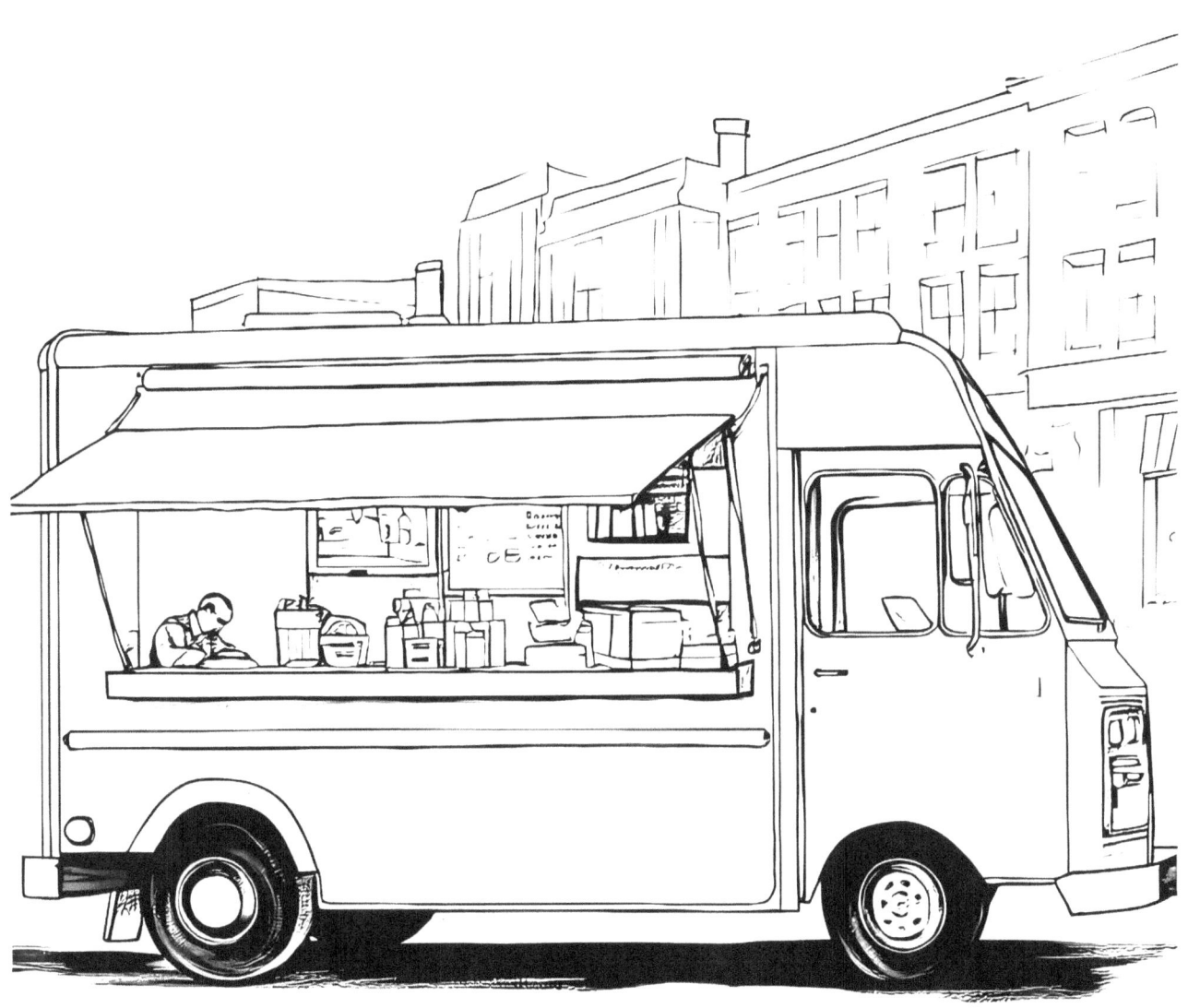

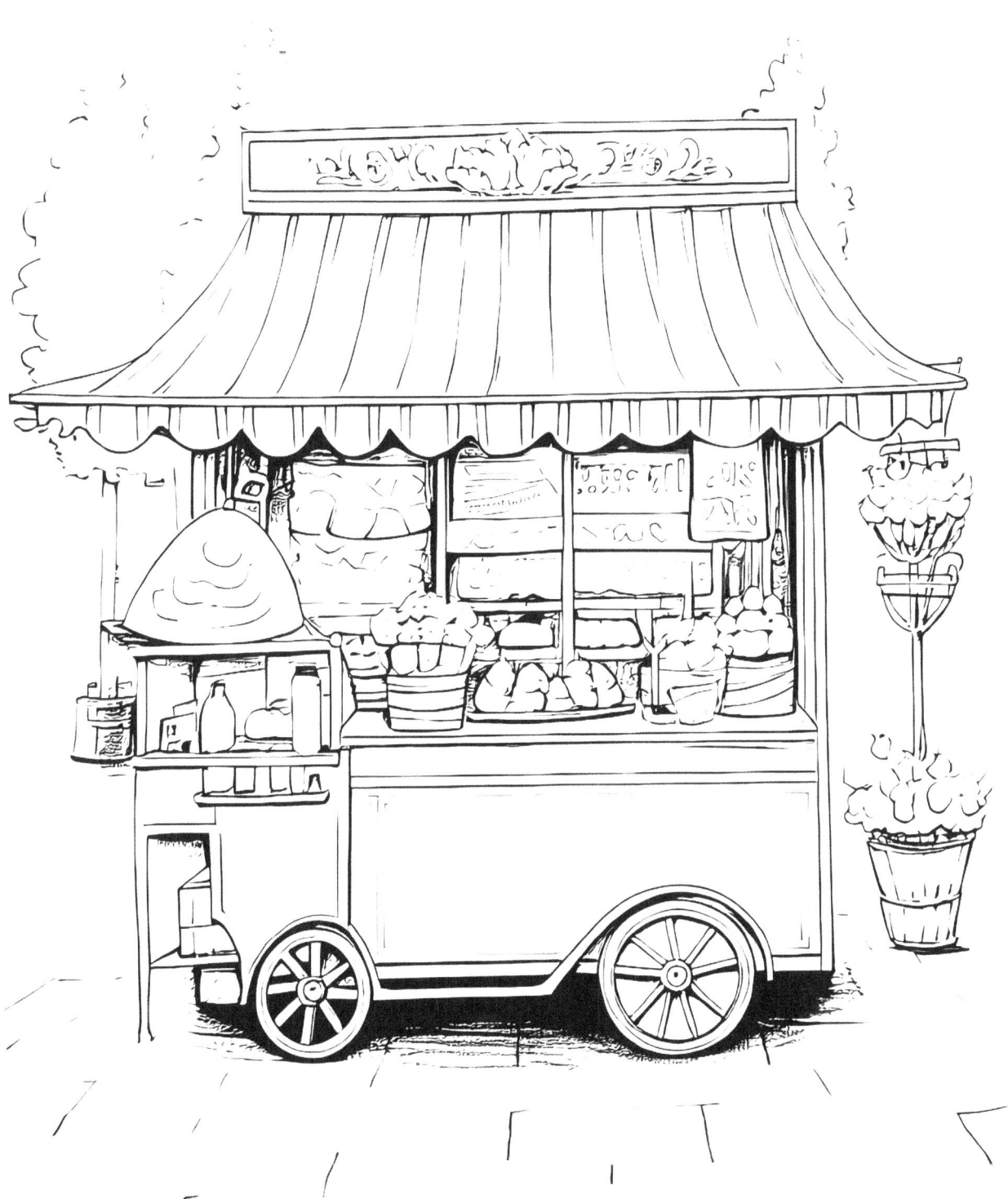

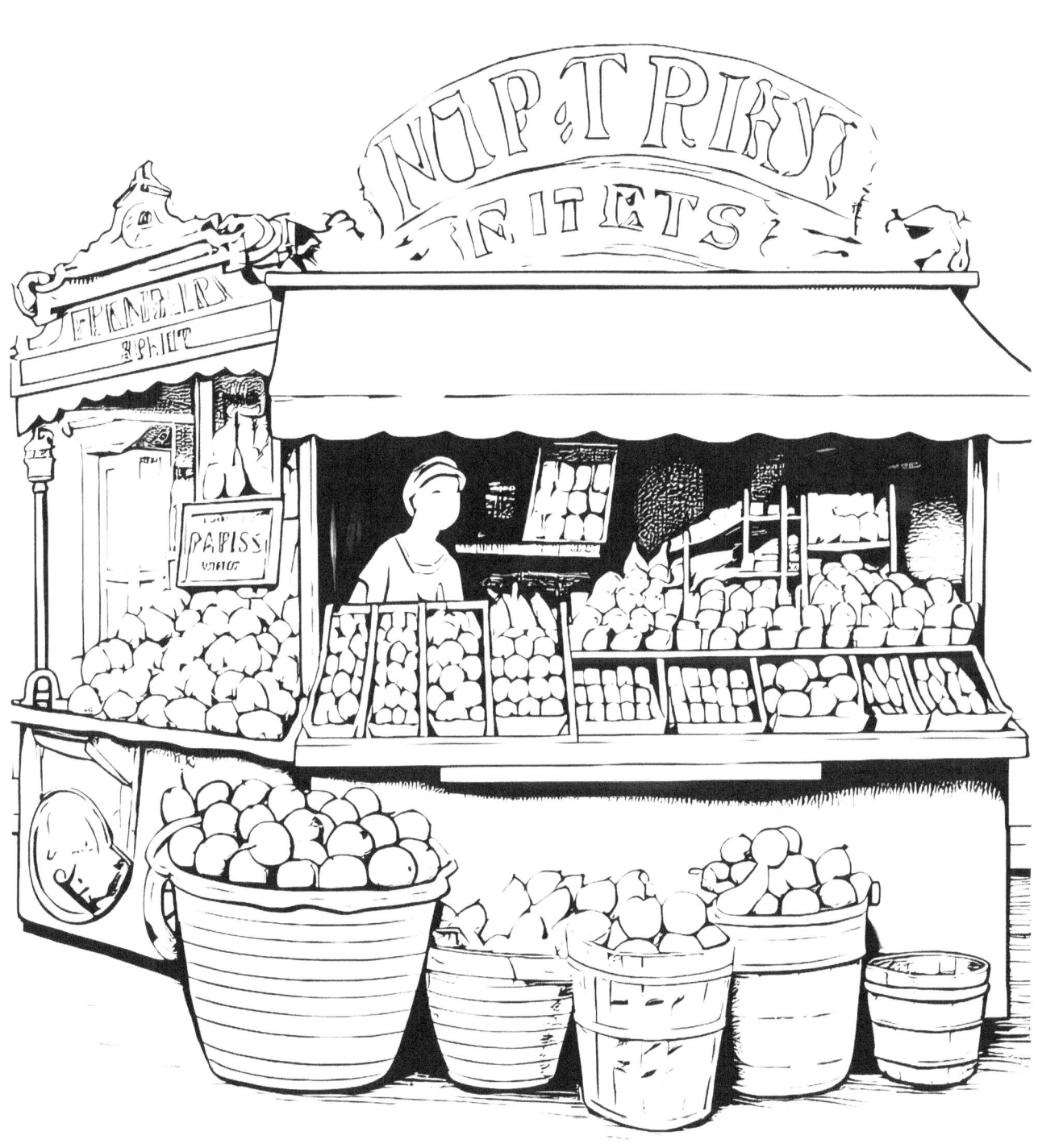

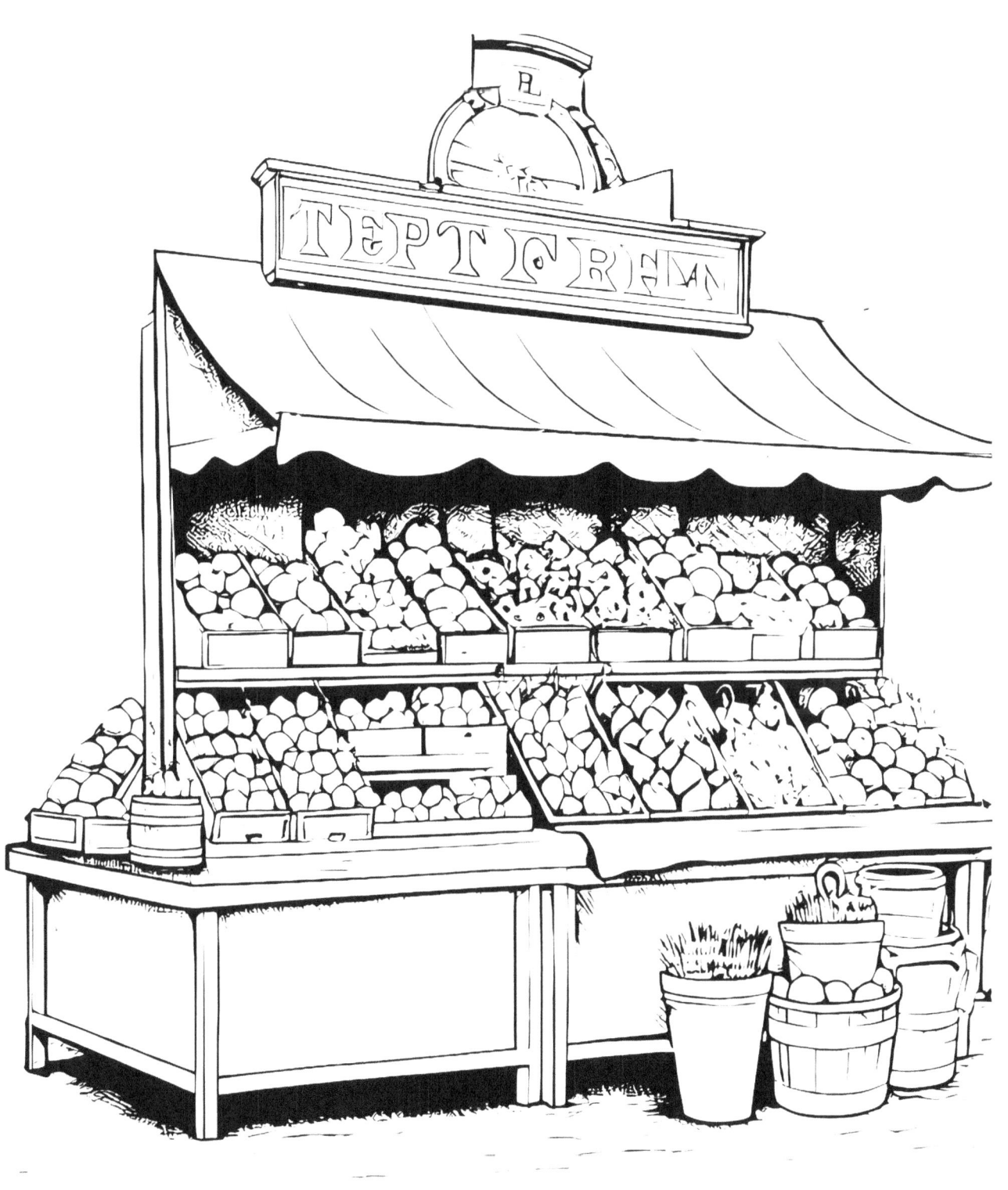

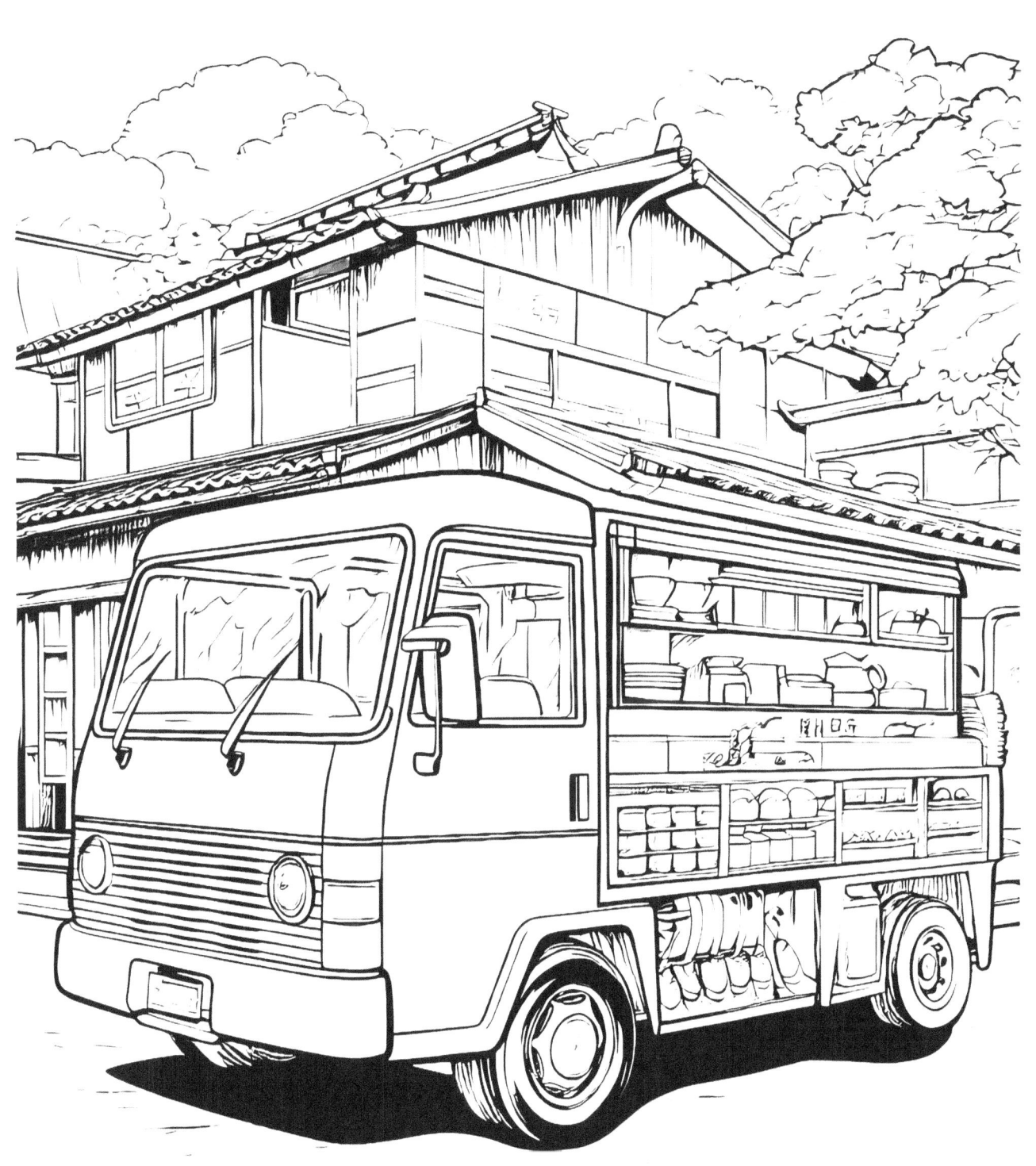

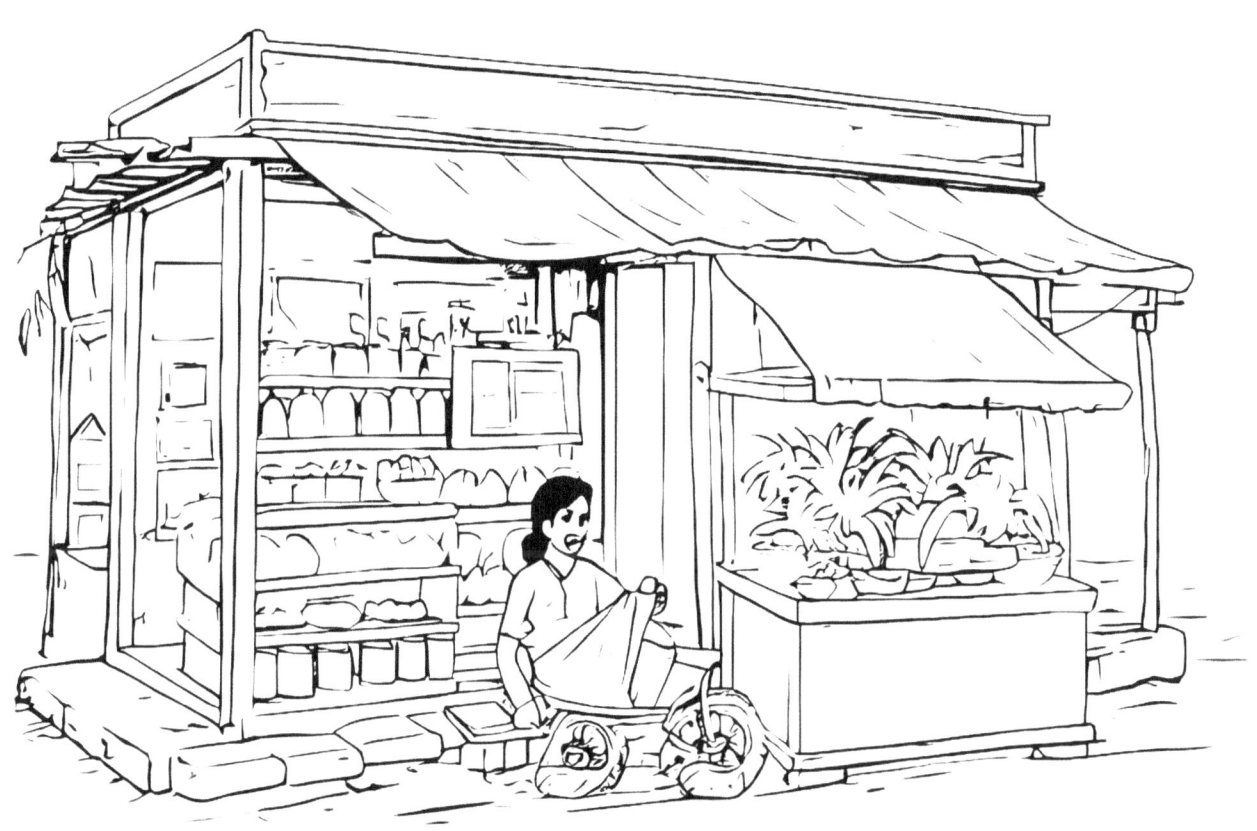

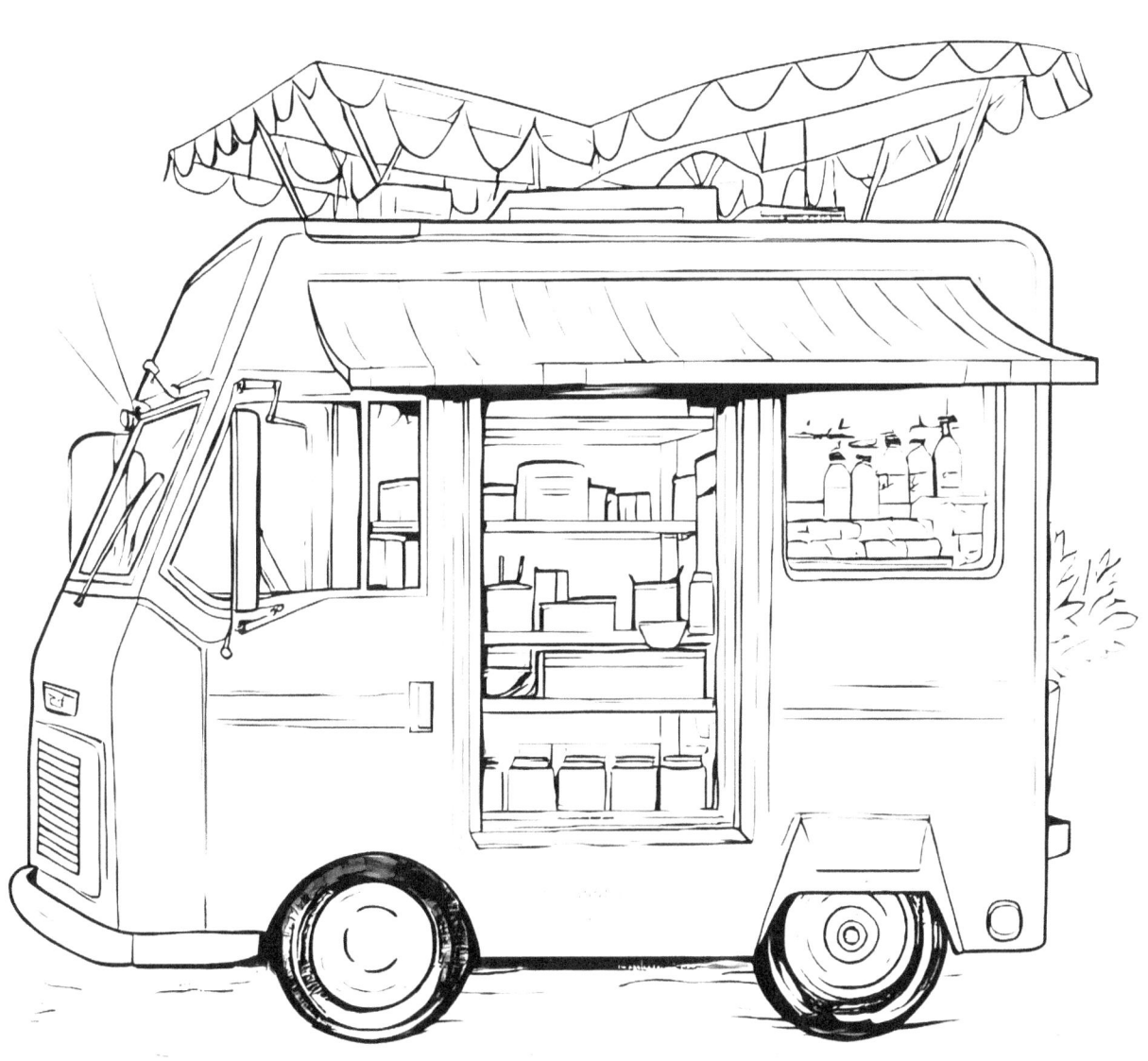

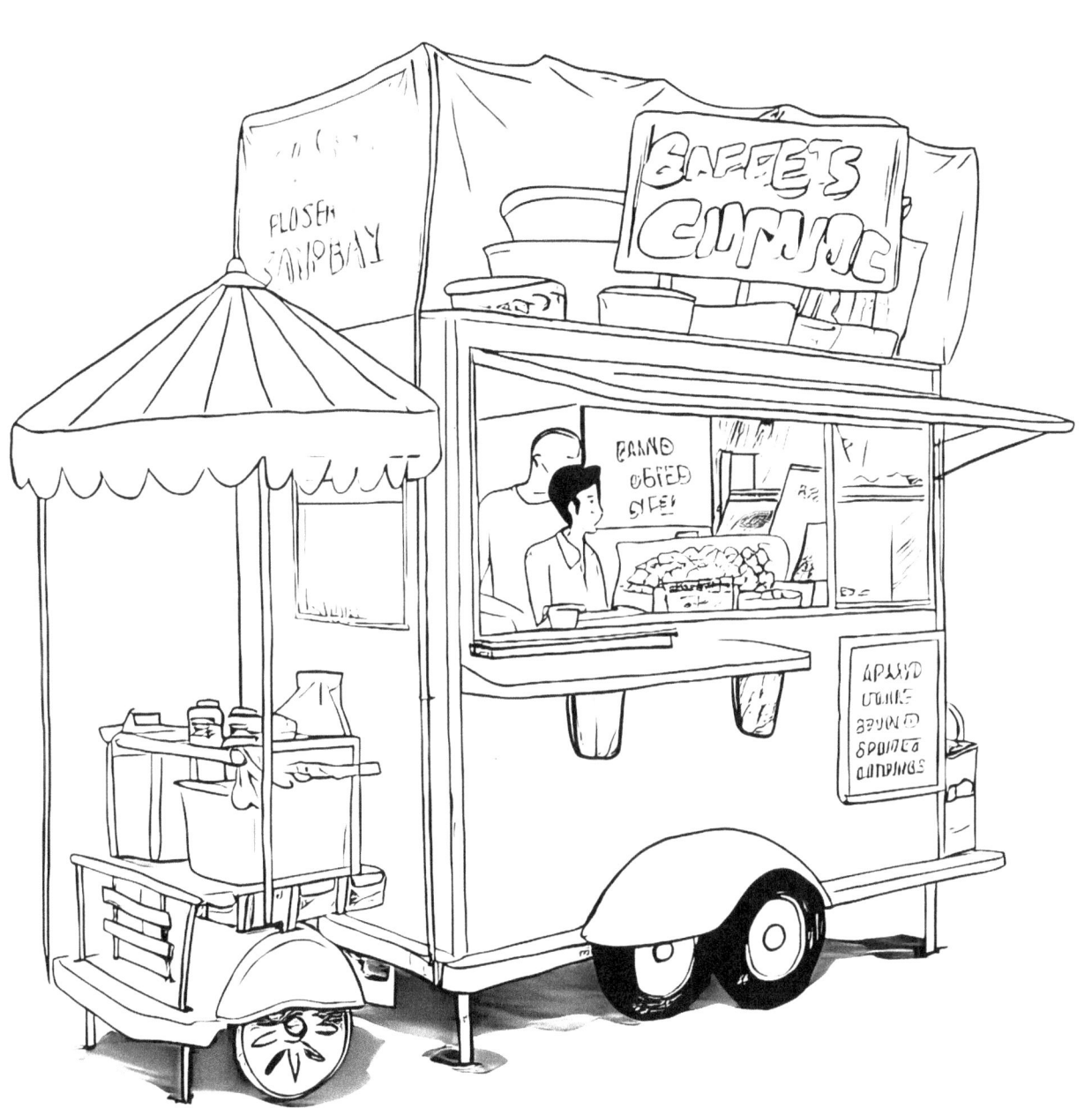

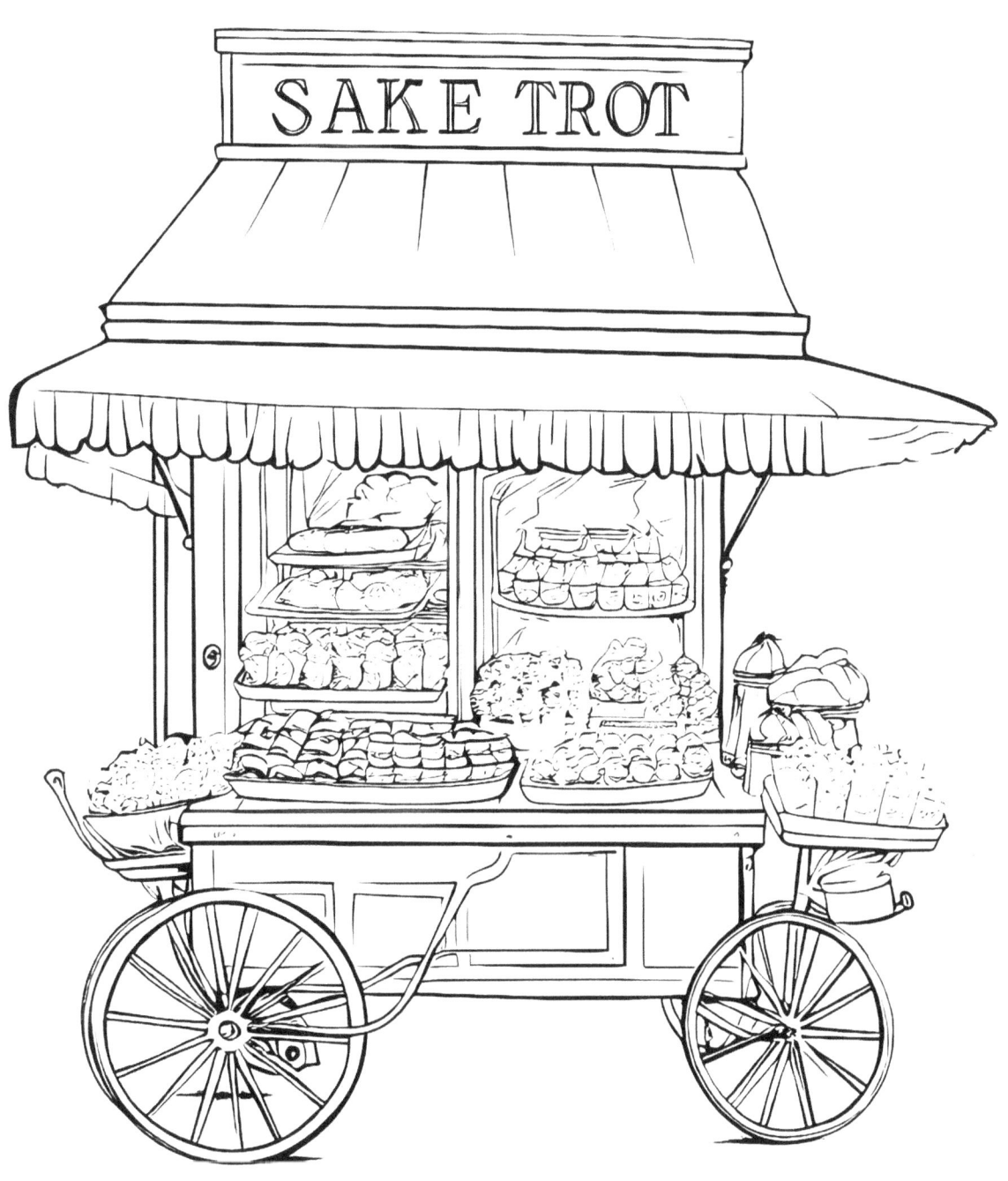

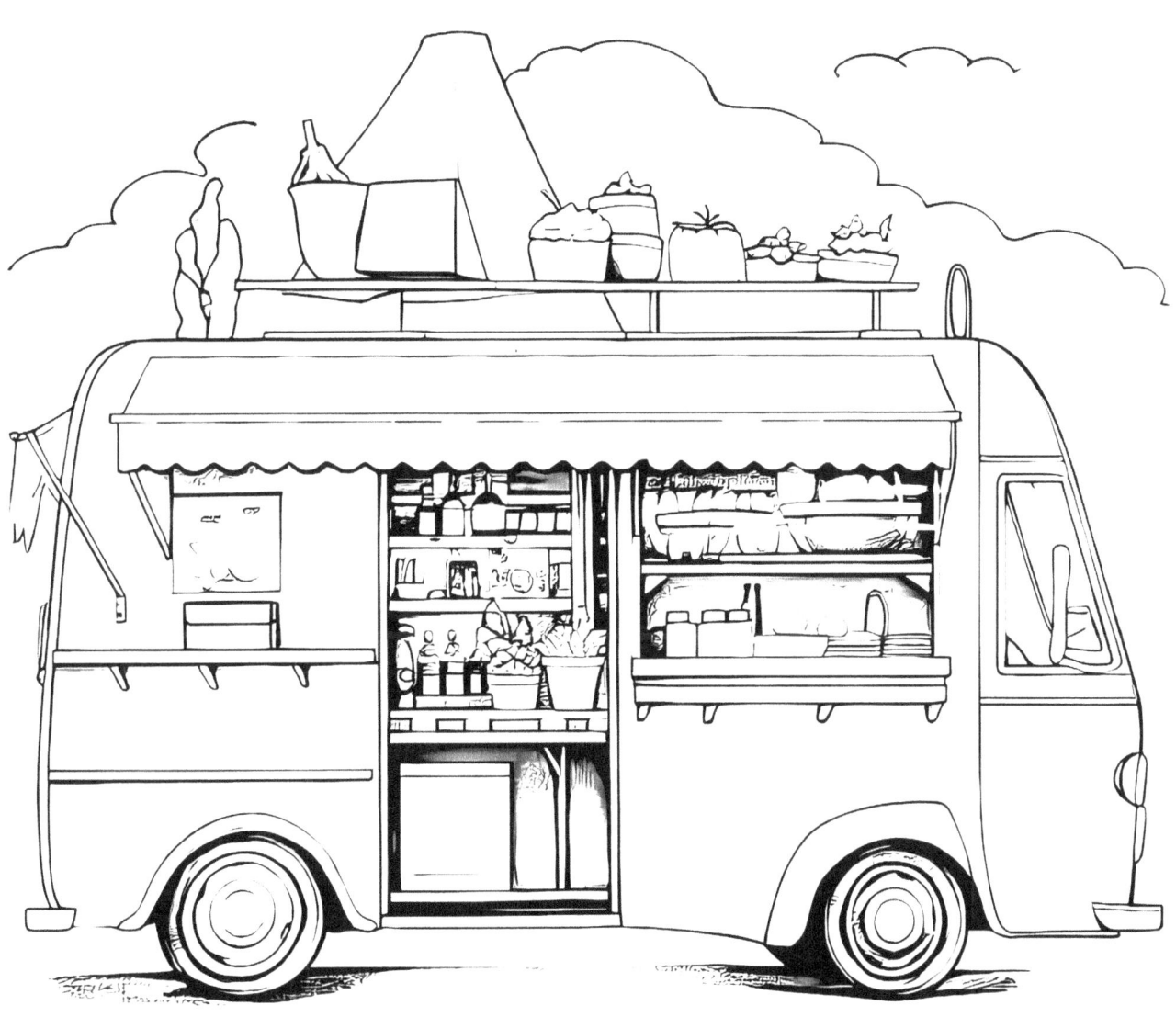

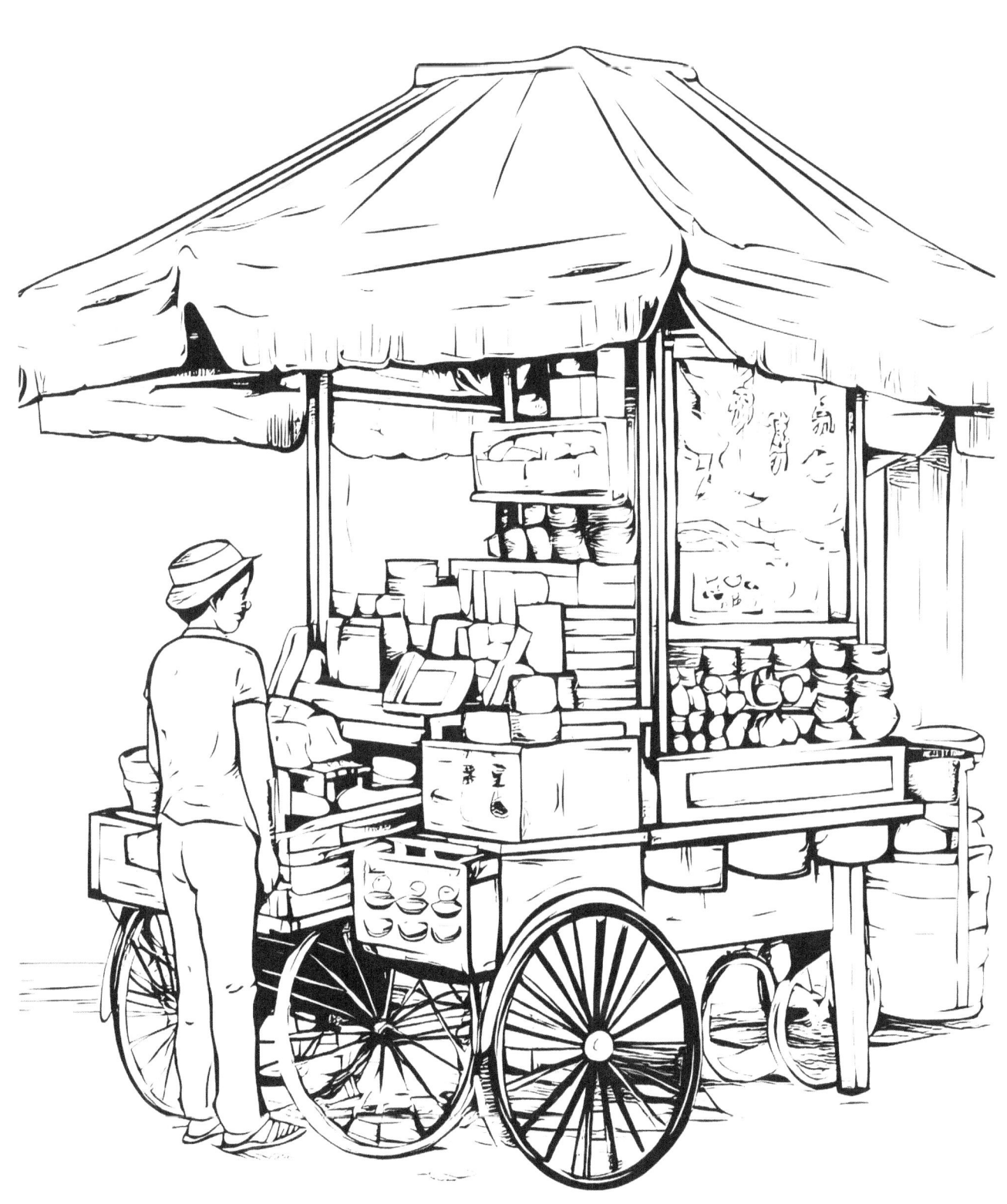

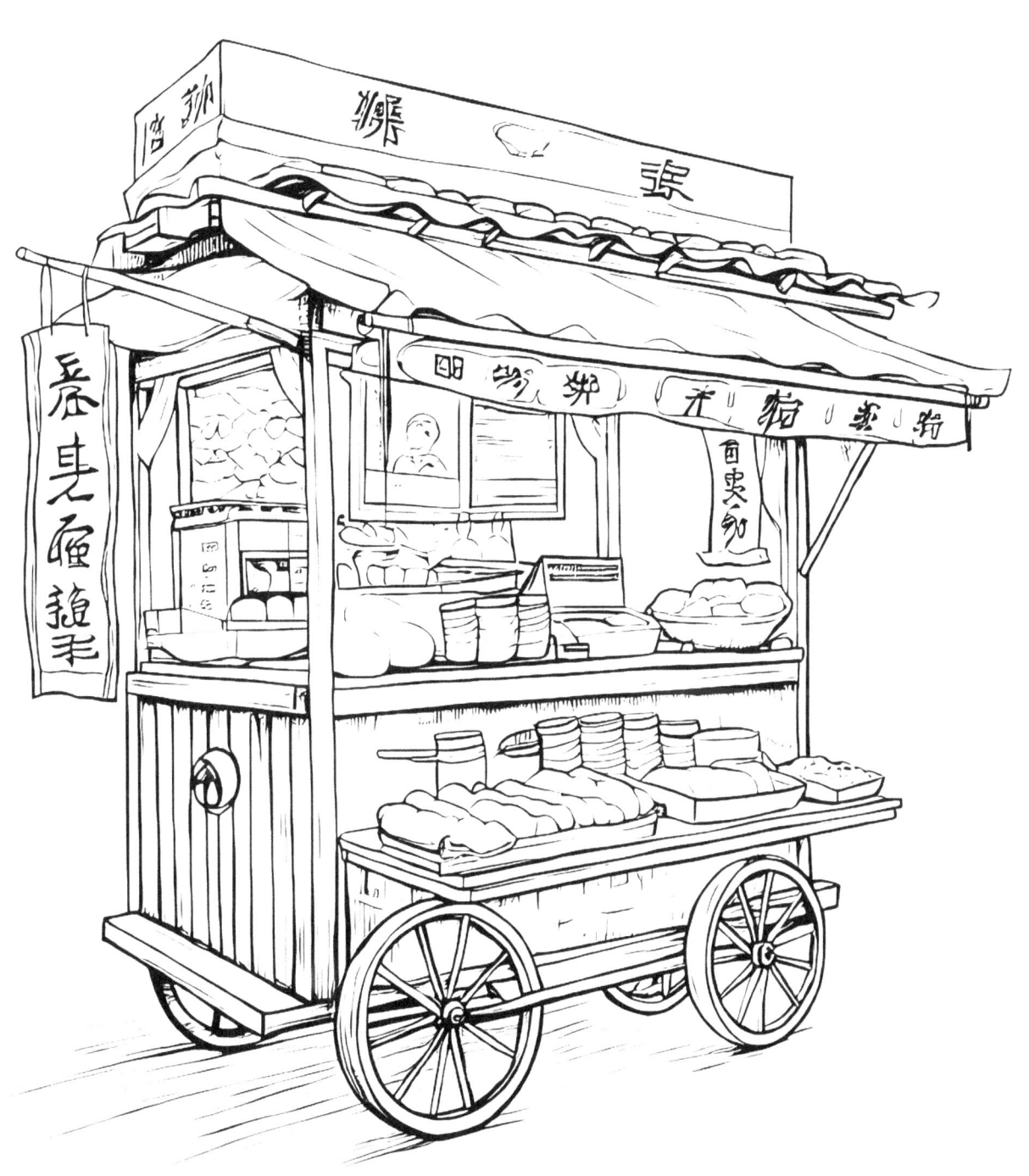

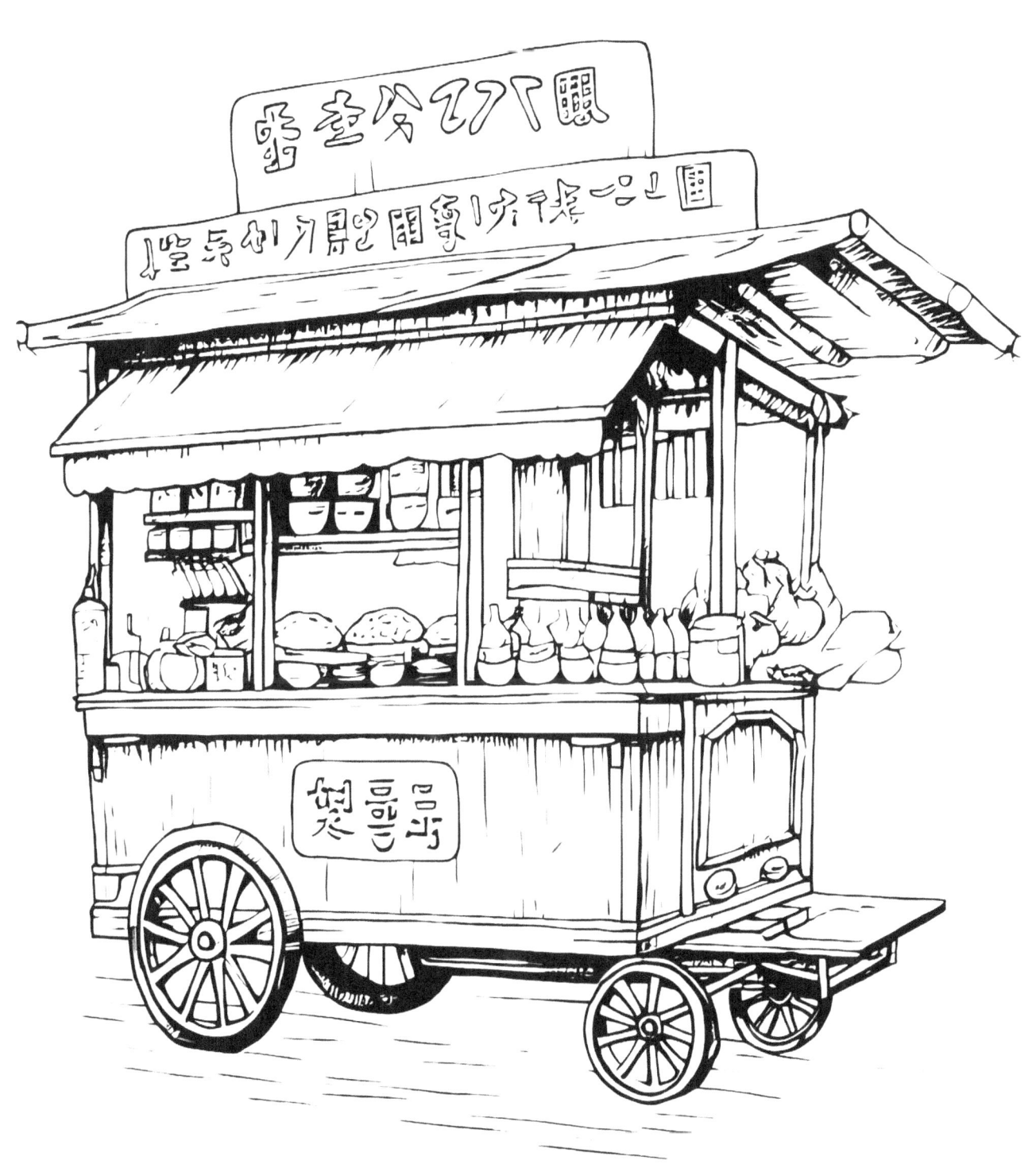

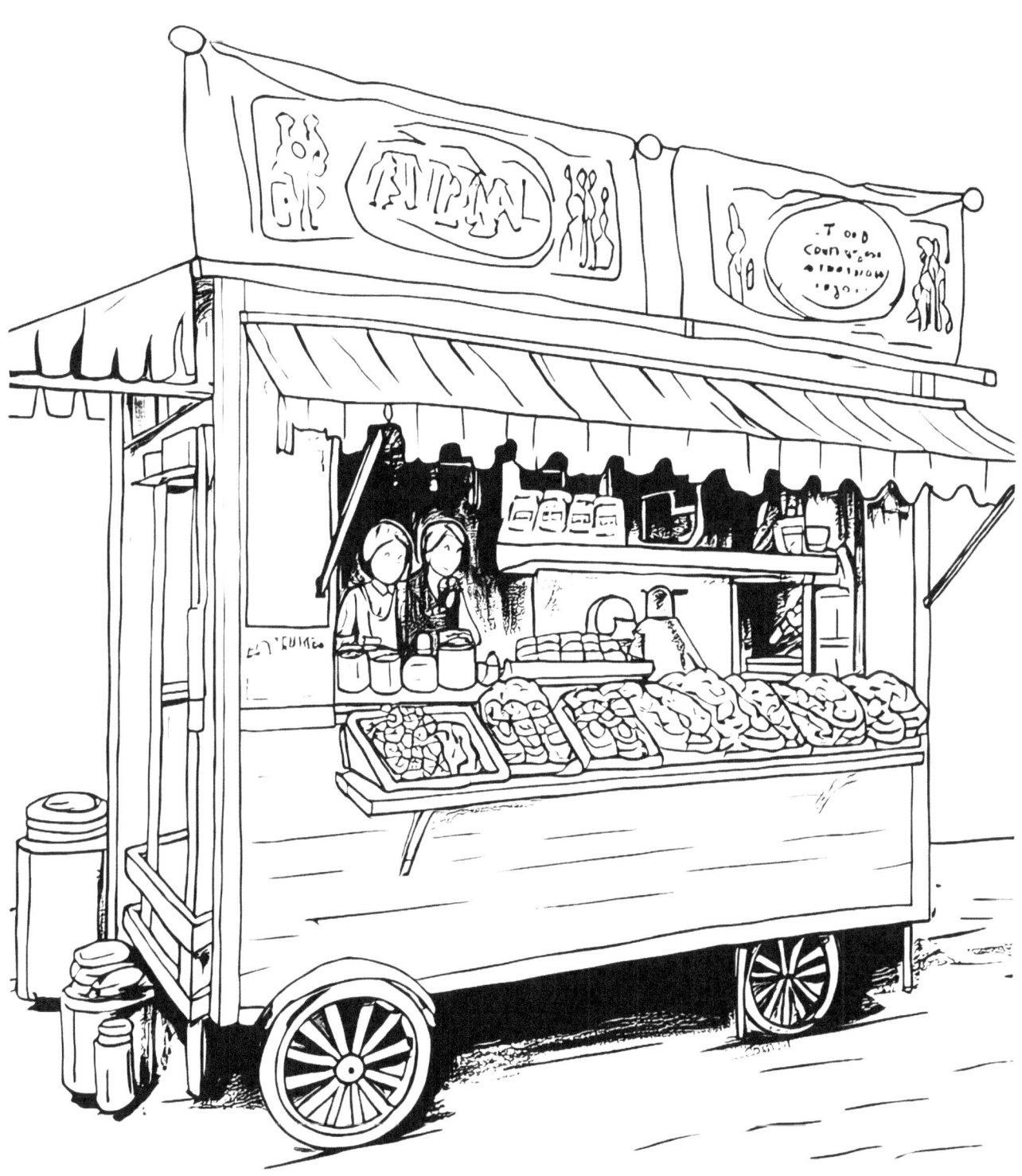

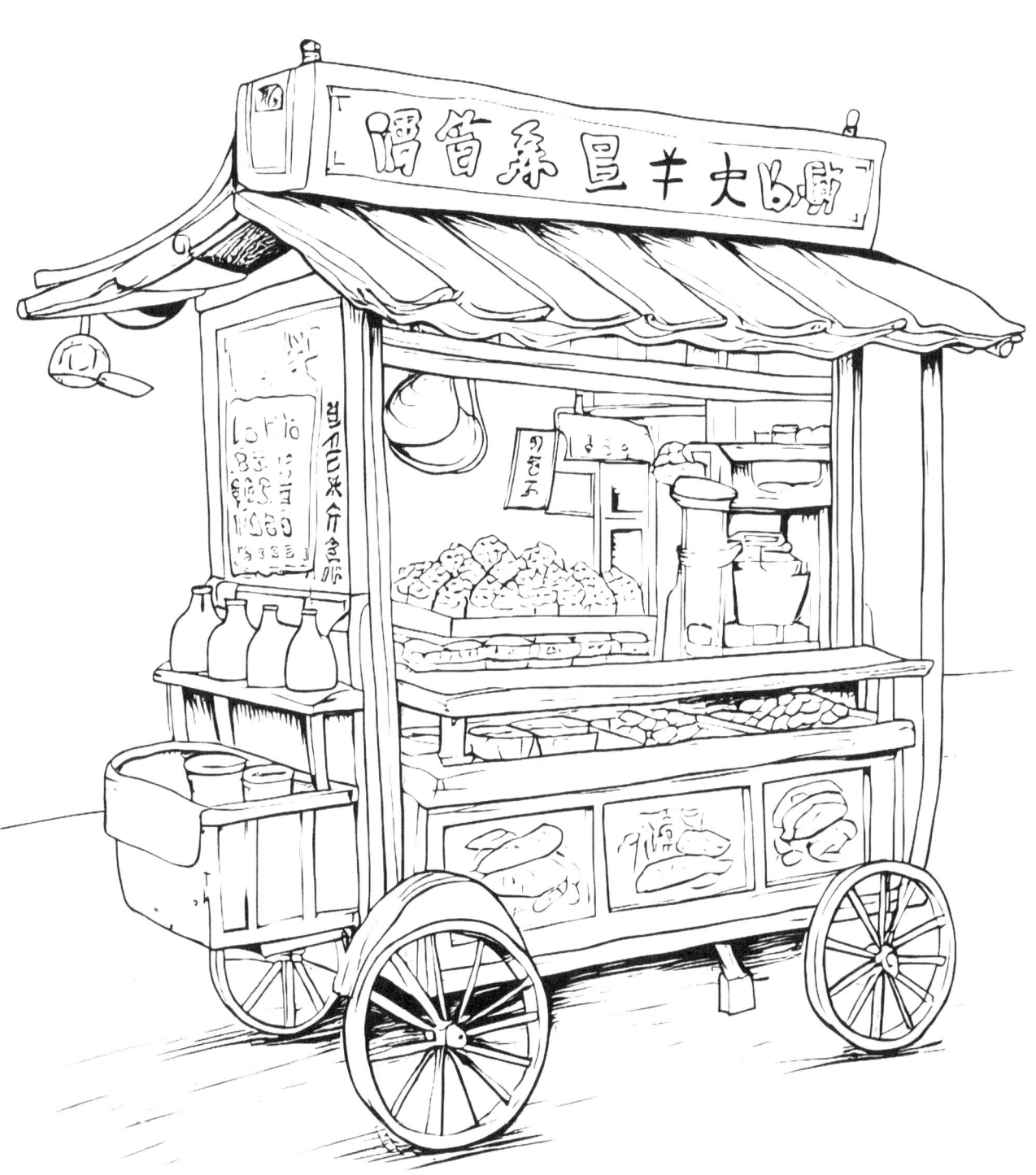

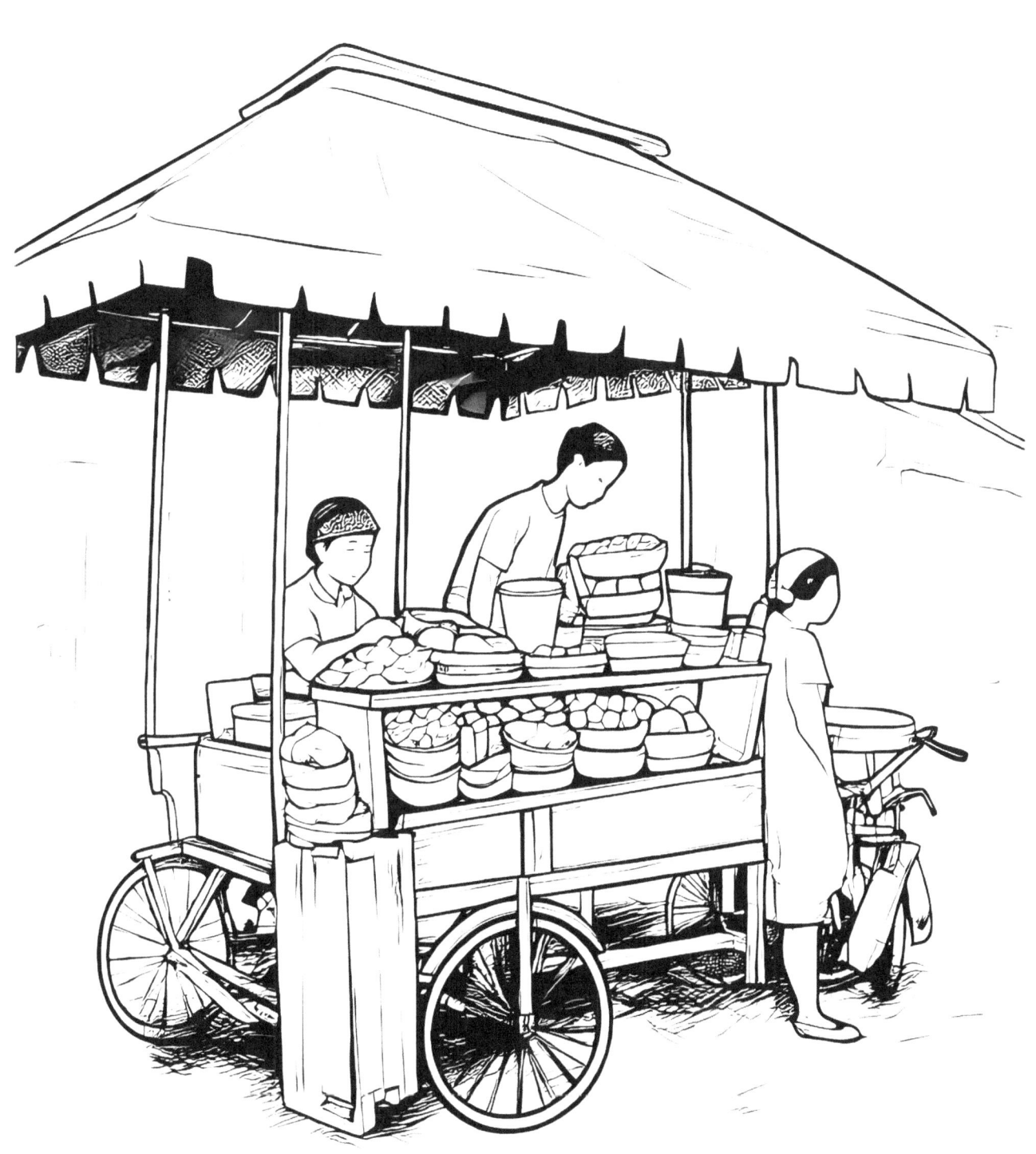

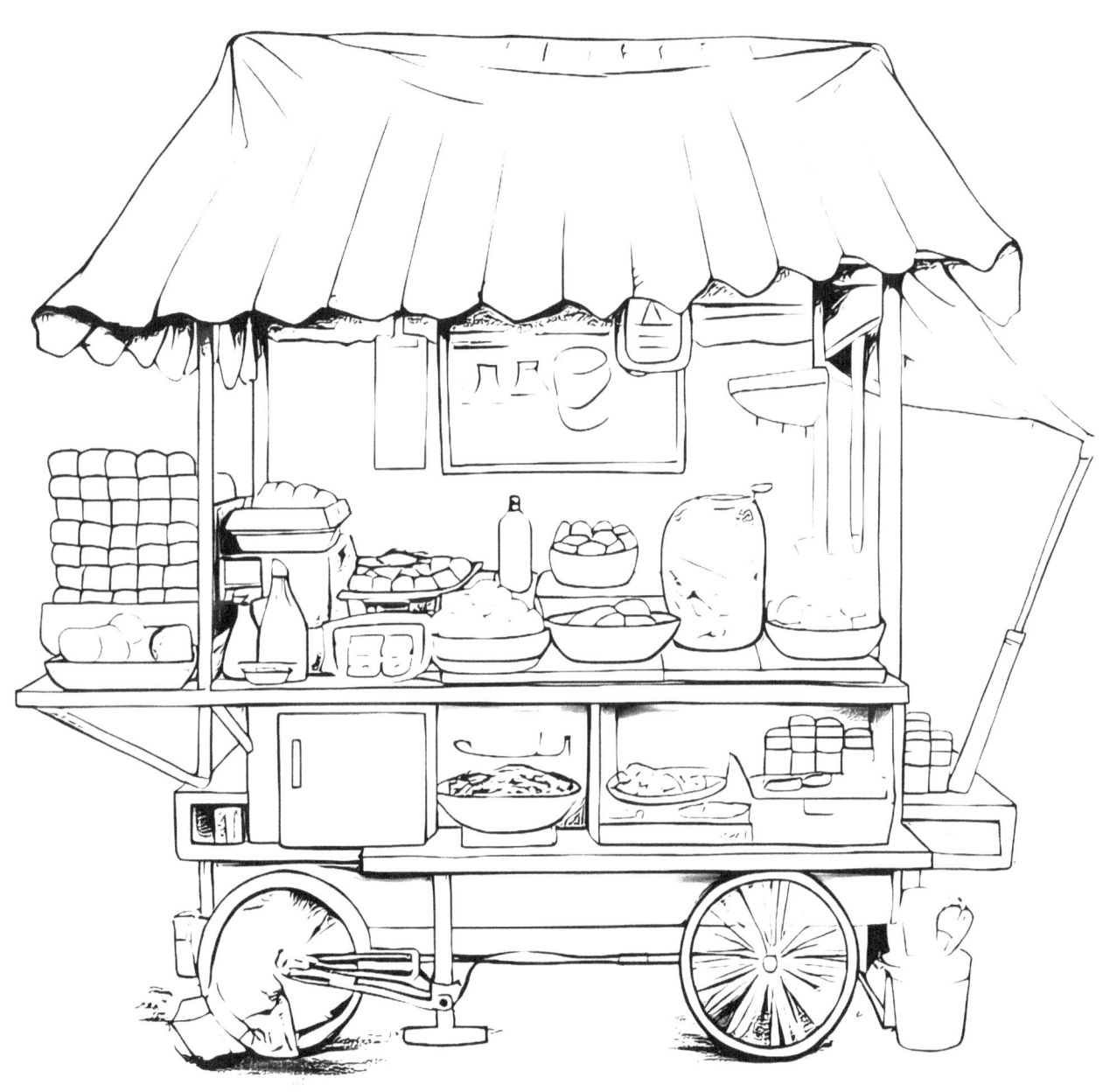

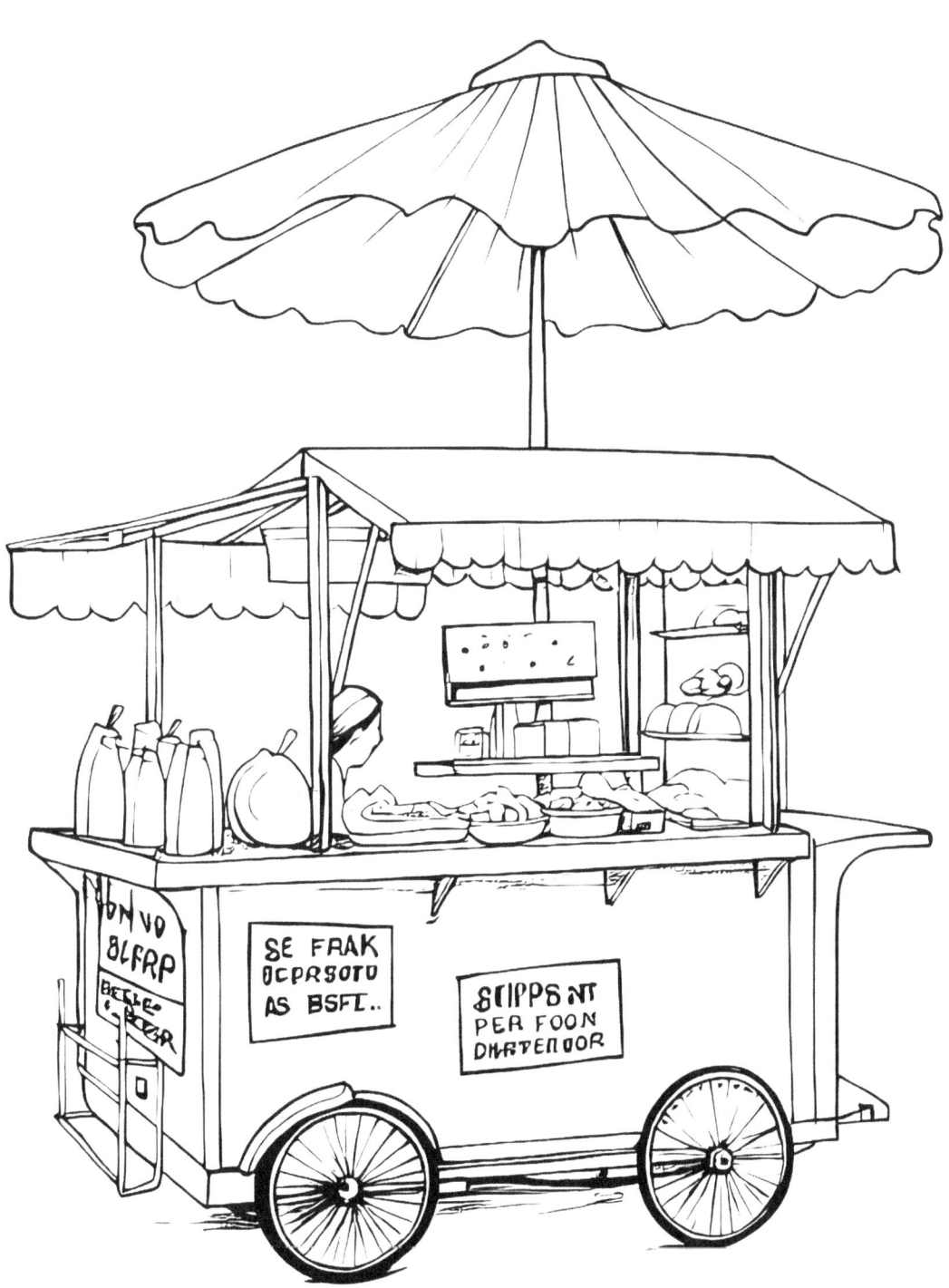

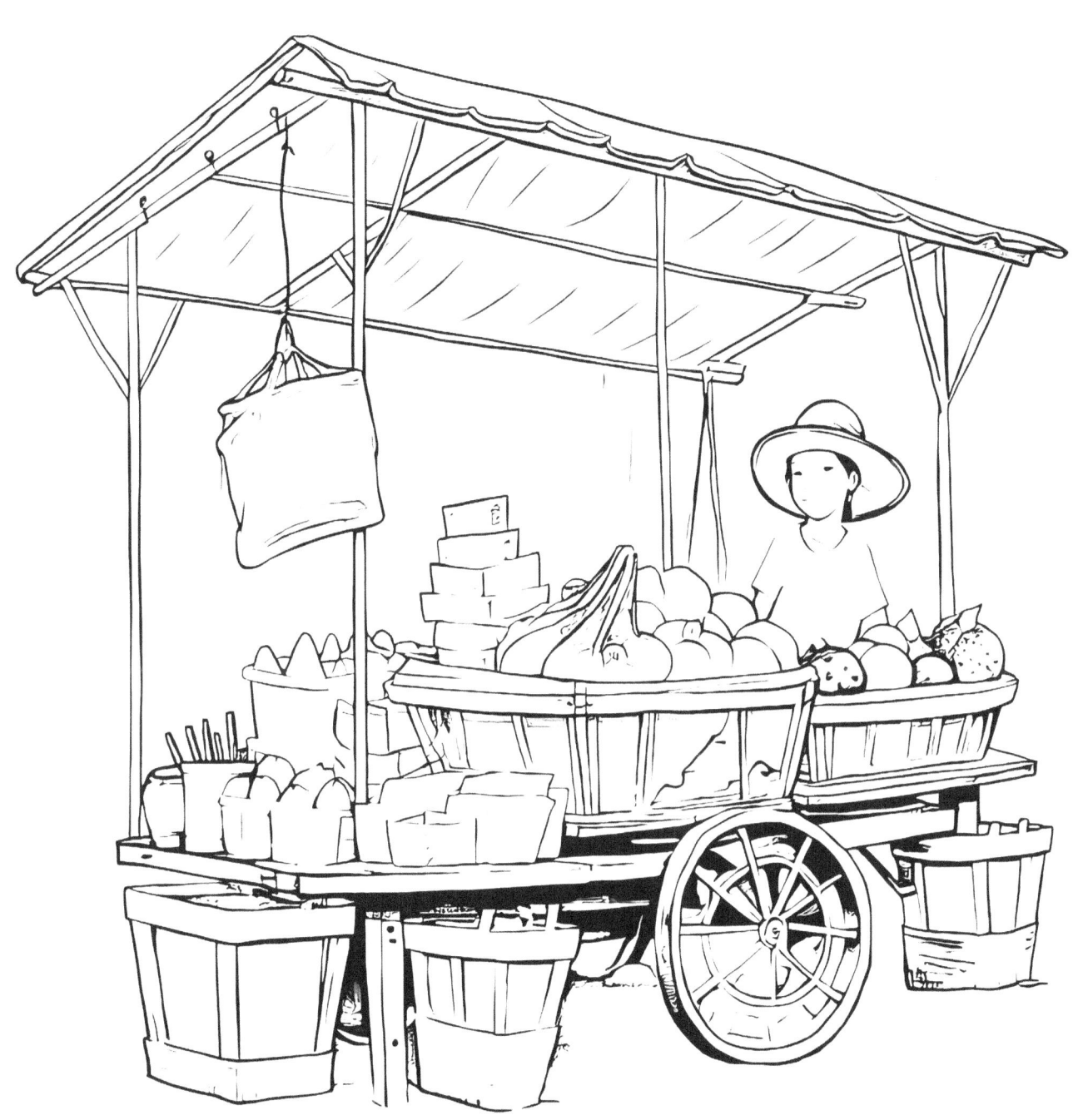

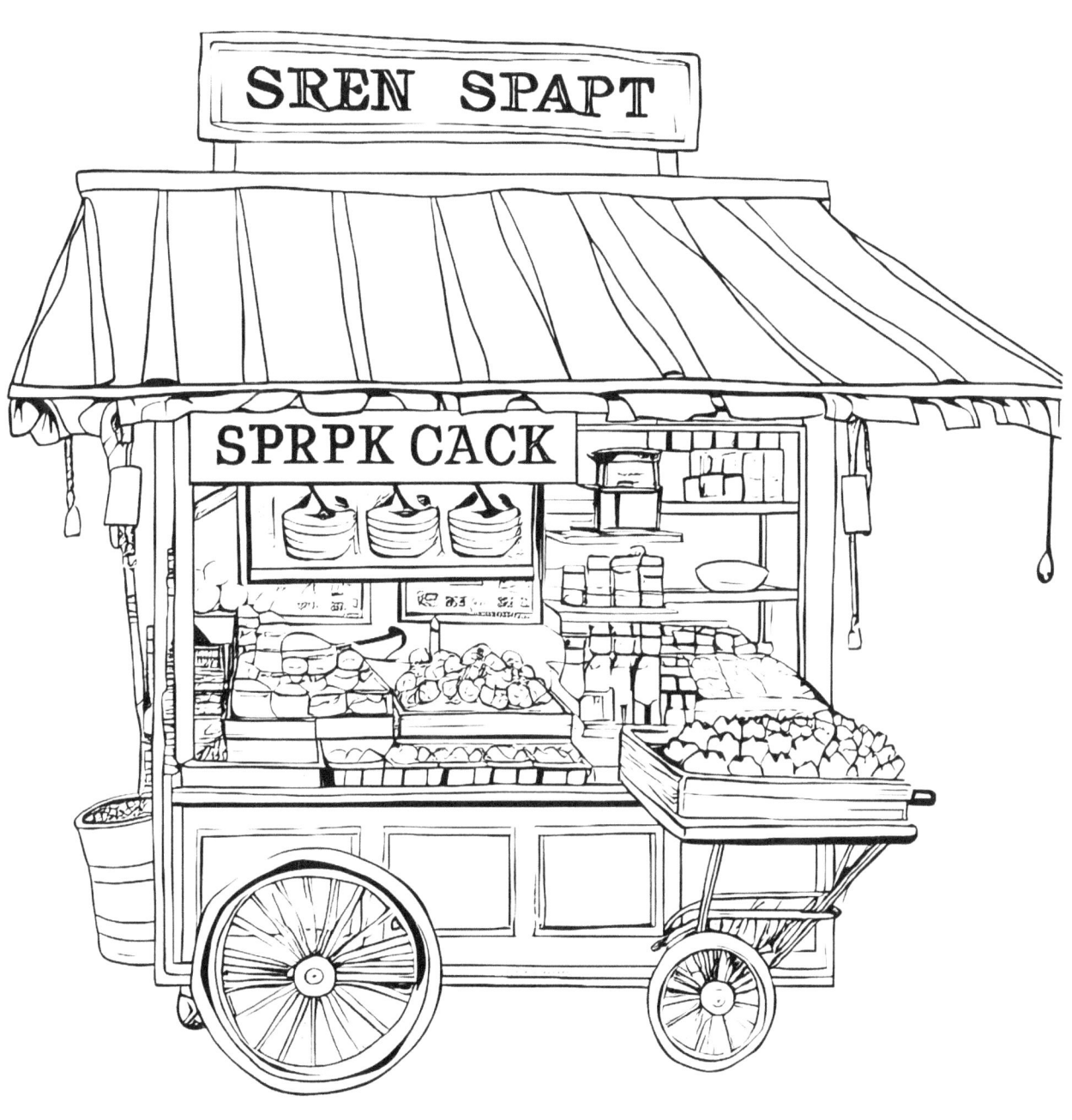

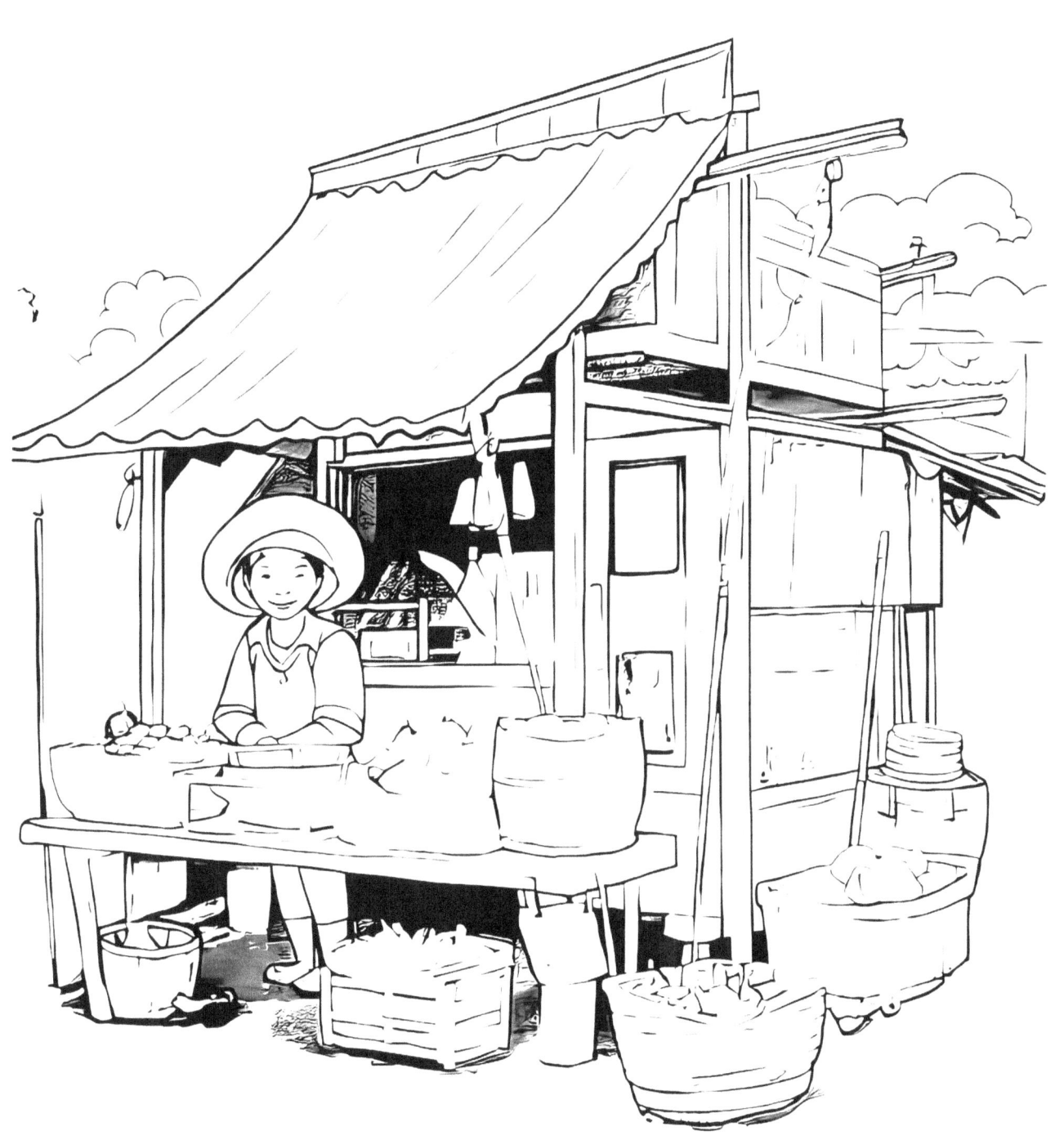

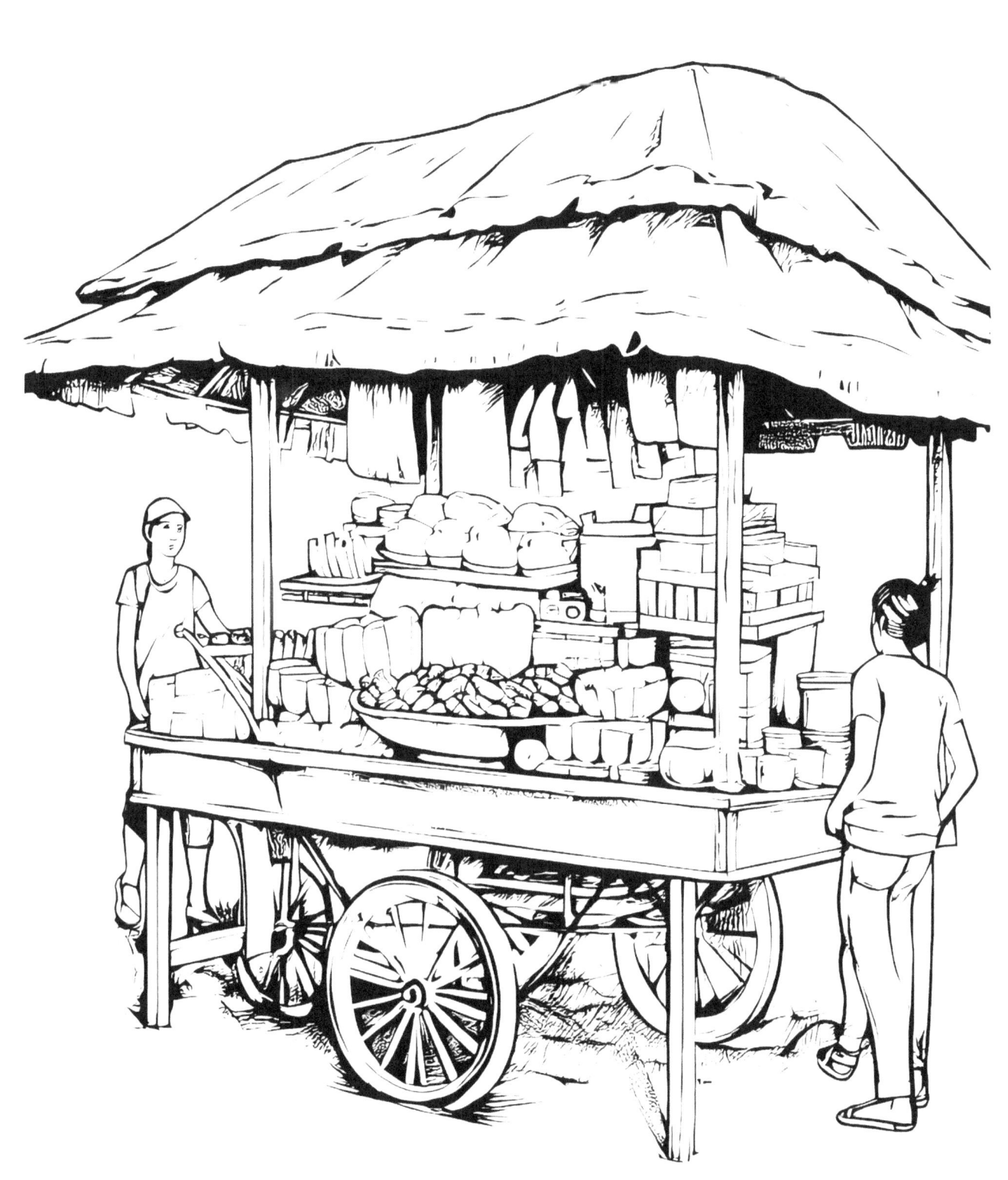

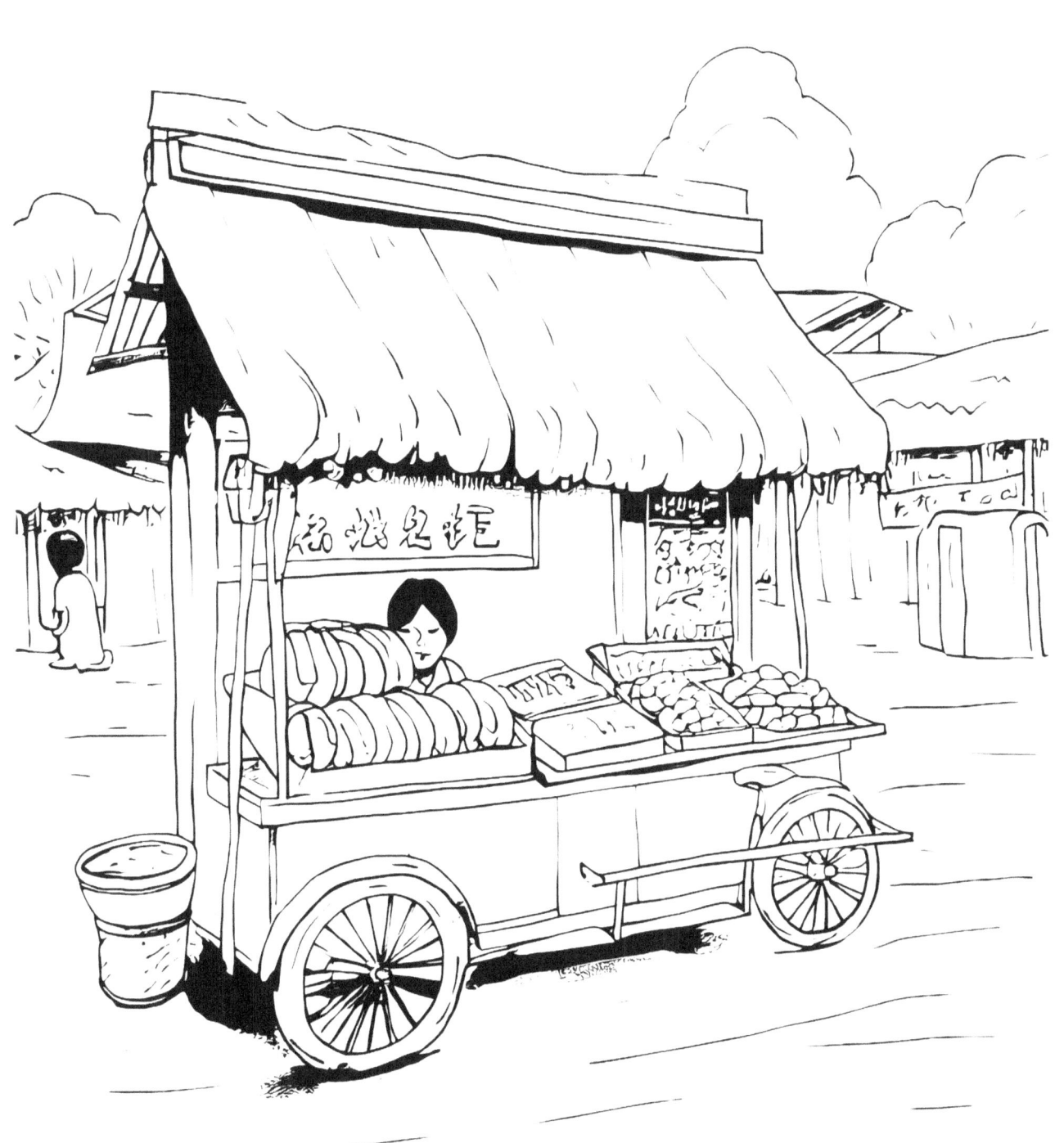

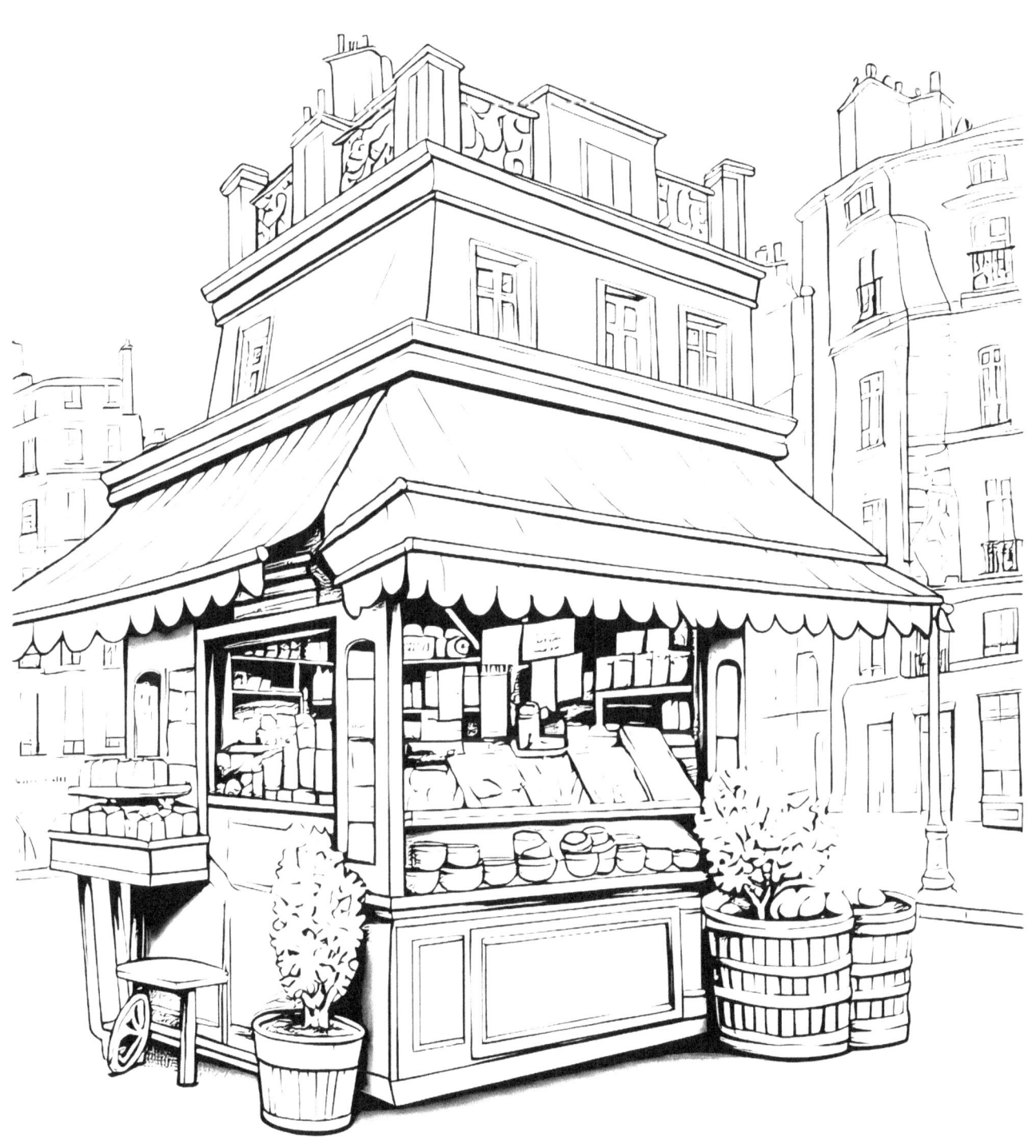